Captive Voices

SOUTHERN MESSENGER POETS

Dave Smith, Series Editor

Captive Voices

NEW AND SELECTED POEMS, 1960–2008

ELEANOR ROSS TAYLOR

With a Foreword by Ellen Bryant Voigt

 LOUISIANA STATE UNIVERSITY PRESS   BATON ROUGE

Published by Louisiana State University Press
Copyright © 2009 by Eleanor Ross Taylor
Foreword copyright © 2009 by Louisiana State University Press
All rights reserved
Manufactured in the United States of America

LSU PRESS PAPERBACK ORIGINAL

Designer: Barbara Neely Bourgoyne
Typeface: Arno Pro

These poems have been selected from *Wilderness of Ladies* (New York: McDowell-Obolensky, 1960), *Welcome Eumenides* (New York: George Braziller, 1972), *New and Selected Poems* (Stuart Wright, 1983), *Days Going/Days Coming Back* (Salt Lake City: University of Utah Press, 1991), and *Late Leisure* (Baton Rouge: Louisiana State University Press, 1999).

Grateful acknowledgment is made to the editors of the following publications, in which some of the new poems first appeared: *Archipelago, Blackbird, Hopkins Review, Hospital Drive.*

Many, many thanks to Dave Smith for causing this book to be born and for guiding it to maturity. Also, thanks to Kaitlin Whitt for putting the physical manuscript together. Special thanks to Eric Gudas for research and valuable advice. Finally, thanks to John Easterly, Catherine Kadair, and Ellen Voigt for bringing it to fruition.

LIBRARY OF CONGRESS CATALOGING-IN-PUBLICATION DATA
Taylor, Eleanor Ross, 1920–
    Captive voices : new and selected poems, 1960–2008 / Eleanor Ross Taylor ; with a foreword by Ellen Bryant Voigt.
        p. cm. — (Southern messenger poets)
    "LSU Press paperback original"—T.p. verso
    ISBN 978-0-8071-3412-2 (pbk. : alk. paper)
    I. Title.
    PS3570.A9285C37 2009
    811'.54—dc22

                                                                      2008042280

The paper in this book meets the guidelines for permanence and durability of the Committee on Production Guidelines for Book Longevity of the Council on Library Resources. ∞

Contents

FOREWORD, by Ellen Bryant Voigt   ix

FROM
Wilderness of Ladies (1960)

    Buck Duke and Mamma   3

    Playing   5

    Wind   7

    Sister   8

    Goodbye Family   10

    The Chain Gang Guard   12

    Night   13

    Woman as Artist   14

    Song   16

    My Grandmother's Virginhood, 1879   17

    Motherhood, 1880   18

    Family Bible   19

FROM
Welcome Eumenides (1972)

    After Twenty Years   27

    Welcome Eumenides   29

    To a Young Writer   36

The Young Writer's Reply   37

Courtesy Call, 1967   38

Flight   39

Epitaph   40

FROM

New and Selected Poems (1983)

The Painted Bridge   43

The Going Away of Young People   45

Women's Terminal Ward   47

New Dust   48

When Robins Return   50

Va. Sun. A.M. Dec. '73   51

Limits   52

To Future Eleanors   53

New Girls   55

The Ribbon to Norwood   56

In Case of Danger   64

Rachel Plummer's Dream   66

In the Bitter Roots   69

FROM

Days Going/Days Coming Back (1991)

At the Altar   73

Short Foray   75

Harvest, 1925   77

Captive Voices   79

Where Somebody Died   83

Maternity Ward   84

Dry Nights   85

No   87

Hatchways   90

Pain in the House   92

Next Year   94

FROM
Late Leisure (1999)

Long-Dreaded Event Takes Place   99

Diary Entry, March 24   100

Overgrown Path   101

Completing the Pilgrimage   102

Te Deum   104

The Lighthouse Keeper   105

Find Me   106

The Accidental Prisoner   107

O Lamp   109

The Diary   110

These Gifts   112

Last Ant   114

Always Reclusive   115

Converse   116

Cocoon   118

Kitchen Fable   119

Late Leisure   120

New Poems (1999–2008)

When to Stop   125

Three Days in Flower   126

Transience   127

Lawrence at the Etruscan Tombs   128

The Dead 129

Gift 130

Two Poems for Randall Jarrell 131

October 132

How to Live in a Trap 133

Our Lives Are Rounded with a Sleep 134

Disappearing Act 135

I See Nobody 136

Laughter 137

Eve 138

Born Alpha 139

Imago Mundi 140

Against the Kitchen Wall 143

Homesick in Paradise 144

De Facto 145

Wrapping Things Up 146

Star 147

Payment Past Due 148

Yes? 149

One Day 150

Ancestral 151

Foreword

IN 1960, INTRODUCING AND PRAISING Eleanor Ross Taylor's first collection of poems, *Wilderness of Ladies,* Randall Jarrell observed that "the world is a cage for women, and inside it the woman is her own cage." It was not a casual insight. A volume of his own poems appeared that same year, and contained this line: "The world goes by my cage and never sees me." The speaker is "The Woman at the Washington Zoo," her "serviceable body" stationed among

> these beings trapped
> As I am trapped but not, themselves, the trap,
> . . .
> Oh, bars of my own body, open, open!

When his book, not hers, received the National Book Award, he regretted the choice in his acceptance speech: that may have been an oblique acknowledgment, and not merely for the double imperative ("Answer! Answer!" she says to a ghost in an early poem). He had inhabited the voices, sensibilities, and emotional dilemmas of women before, finding through these a way to "express a range of being from gentility to catatonia," as he said of Taylor's subjects and images, an apt characterization of his own earlier "Seele im Raum." In 1960, though, and again in his 1965 collection of poems, the figure had become more explicitly sexualized:

> For so many years
> I was good enough to eat; the world looked at me
> And its mouth watered.

It is not far-fetched to presume that Jarrell, the older, more accomplished poet, took some sort of permission from Taylor, something not yet, in midcentury America, readily available anywhere else: "[No poems] come more naturally out of a woman's ordinary existence, take both their subjects and their images out of the daily and nightly texture of her life." His introduction to *Wilderness of Ladies* also noted a signature dichotomy of style: "The violent emotion of so much of [Taylor's] poetry would be intolerable except for the calm matter-of-factness, the seriousness and plain truth, of so much else; and except for the fact that this despairing extremity is resisted by her, forced from her." One can almost catch out the twentieth century's canniest reader of poetry as he formulates the aesthetic, the redeployment of vision and gifts, for his last great volume of poems, *The Lost World*.

An introduction has a large advantage. Jarrell's reported potential, and used forebears (Hardy and Dickinson) to measure it; this current opportunity, for a life's work, reports achievement, and uses poets indebted to her; but within each introduction, there is the firm conviction that her poetry is *sui generis*, which must be proved on the reader's pulse. After these pages, you will see first-hand the extreme compression, the teasing shards of narrative, the haunting, disjunctive lyric images, the swift moves from sly indirection to clenched-teeth irony to confrontation, the interleaving of exact speech and the unspeakable.

Much of that exact speech—Taylor's diction and syntax—is highly idio-syncratic; much of it, especially in dialogue, is deliberately Southern, the idiom of the Piedmont. But their strategies belong to another, larger species. In rural Vermont, one frequently hears an eloquent shorthand in local exchanges. A woman is speaking, and includes without noun referent the masculine pro-noun: "*He* likes his fish fried," or, "*He* got done at the quarry this fall." Whether the information is small bore or large, the tacit assumption, about the iden-tity of that "He," mythologizes. It dramatizes power. If the listener is a man, proper deference has been given, a dog exposing its belly to the alpha dog. If the listener is a woman, volumes of back-story mumble underneath, material too volatile, perhaps too incriminating, to be made explicit:

> ... so much in it
> ... dangerous on the playground,
> too good for everyday,
> ... those splendid fireworks
> hazardous to institutions
> (from "At the Altar")

The reluctance is a tactic for survival, not coyness or camouflage. As Taylor says of "The Diary,"

The more I "Speak up, girl!"
the less it says outright,
wants in fact to not say.

Richard Howard has noticed that "Taylor devised . . . and practices still, for all the modesty of her address, a tough modernist poetics of fragmentation and erasure." And Taylor herself, in a review of Sylvia Plath's *Ariel* in 1967, claimed as the "chief pleasure of poetry . . . the feeling of having come upon a silence, a privacy, upon intellect existing unselfconsciously somewhere out of reach of [the] camera." At the same time, "Find Me" points us to

> . . . my trail of fragments,
>   stale crumbs,
>
>   green broken boughs
>   of protocol.
>   Footprints
> . . .
>
>   tatters of sackcloth
>   on the undergrowth

In Taylor's work, with every choice that moves the central sensibility "out of reach of [the] camera," choices of diction and detail simultaneously imply the rich, complex sensibility *behind* the camera, not despite but because of "the modesty of her address." Lines like these suggest through their tone what has been withheld:

> A husband, more or less!
> A family, more or less!—
>   (from "Sister")

Adrienne Rich has called Eleanor Ross Taylor's style "a style born of tension, in which whispered undertones are in dialogue with the givens of social existence, with the sudden explosive burst of rebellion or recognition." The rebellion usually comes under cover of persona; the recognition is everywhere present, from the tightest small lyric to the capacious histories. Rich again, praising "Welcome Eumenides": "What I find compelling . . . , besides the authority and originality of her language, is the underlying sense of how the conflicts of imaginative and intelligent women have driven them on, lashed them into genius or madness, how the home-nursing, the household administration, the patience and skill in relationships acquired at such expense in a family-centered life, became an essential part of the strength of a woman like [Florence] Nightingale, but at tremendous price." Here's how Rich phrases it in her own poem about Marie Curie: "Her wounds came from the same source as her power."

Taylor characterizes her later poetry as "involved with my own ghost." The family-centered life allowed in most explicitly is rural, poor, Methodist, and literate. The Ross farm had no running water or electricity but plenty of Scripture and schoolbooks and the nineteenth- century popular novels her father brought home, borrowed from prosperous friends. All four siblings—two older brothers (James Ross and Fred Ross), her younger sister Jean Ross (married to poet Donald Justice), and Eleanor too—would write and publish fiction. All four went to college.

In 1936, when she was sixteen, what was available to Eleanor, through loans and jobs at the dining hall and library, was the University of North Carolina's branch for women in Greensboro. She studied there with Allen Tate and Caroline Gordon and, after a year teaching at a country school, pursued her fiction at Vanderbilt. While in Nashville, Eleanor spent holidays with the couple in Monteagle, where they had rented a large cottage with Robert Lowell and Jean Stafford. At Easter, 1943, she was introduced to another visitor, another young fiction writer, Lowell's (and Jarrell's) friend from Kenyon College, on furlough from the army. She was already betrothed to someone else, but a few months later, on June 4, Eleanor Ross and Peter Taylor were married at the cottage, over the objections of both families.

That's a high-stakes romantic premise, and the consequences of it enough to make "[t]he female bitter black tongues hum." There was no well-worn path back to the small Cedar Grove community of Norwood, North Carolina, from New York City, London, Paris, Rapallo, Cambridge, Columbus, or Charlottesville, VA, where Peter's academic career settled him in at the university in 1967 (and where his widow still lives), with additional houses in Sewanee, Tennessee, and Gainesville, Florida. A daughter was added to the household in 1948, a son in 1955, and soon, Peter's steadily increasing fame. Apparently, there wasn't time enough, or room enough, for matched ambition. "You have to hand it to him," she has said, "he stuck to his guns from the very first. Our daughter Katie was taught not to rattle that knob to his study door."

But Shakespeare's sister, or Peter Taylor's wife, could compress the energy of her fiction into the high-tension space of her poems. The use of voice to establish character, a Hardyesque connection to a region, a compressed or elided plot line, an abundance of observed detail and historical reference—we can trace a narrative impulse, rescued and redirected. And there was one singular recompense. Peter's first teaching job was at the Women's College in Greensboro, with Jarrell, and in 1947 the two old friends moved their families into adjoining duplex apartments, where "Peter . . . made me show Randall those first poems." He was a close friend to both Taylors until he died, and a champion for Eleanor, cajoling her onto the page and into publication.

Selections from Taylor's five books of poetry are now gathered together, with a generous group of new pieces, into this essential volume. It will be no surprise to find so many pioneers embodied here, since she herself is one (though we can safely assume she doesn't see herself that way); "To me," her poem "The Diary" tells us; "They write to me." Among all these "Captive Voices," retrieved from the silence and erasure of history, none is more indelible than the middle-aged woman traveling south, following a "Ribbon to Norwood" to visit her dying mother, retracing Ariadne's "thread of generations." At the farm in Cedar Grove, the "he" at the center is long gone, but "Here are the rubbed dust wallows,/the burrowing coiling to the labyrinth."

In the poems, in the life: "Shall I hum? Or sing/out clear?" After fifty years, perhaps we've learned how to read these trails of ribbon and thread, breadcrumbs and bent-back branches: they take us straight to the Interior.

ELLEN BRYANT VOIGT
August, 2008

Wilderness of Ladies

(1960)

Buck Duke and Mamma

He came bringing us a milkpail full
Of speckled, wild, gooseplums—
All fat unsmelt-out perfumedom—
And perched on the back porch curb to taste a few.
"Sour! Your eyes'll water, Miss Tempe!
But sweet, too."
Mamma's way was posing by the silent pool
And tossing in the line amiss
That shook the skies of the other world
And all but loosed the roots of this.
She trimmed and trained the roundabout backwoods,
Was glad that Buck Duke had a devilish eye;
It saved an orphan from dire fortitude,
And saved his grandpa's house from sanctity.
"Your Papa doesn't favor your going there.
I say, enter evil to cure evil, if you dare!"
As she went about her cast-off household chores
She overlooked them with a lavish bow
Inspired by that heroine of poems,
Her elocution teacher, Miss Hattie Yow.
        "Nothing to do? In this world of ours?
        Where weeds spring daily amidst sweet flowers?"
        Your-mammy-never-came-to-much-my-Buck.

"Don't drink that Mackling Spring's brack water
Whe'r it's high or low.
The cows stand in there and let go."
But old Duke's beardy words were moss for campfire
When they took their kitchen rations to the woods.
Mamma's boys looked out for sassafras, but Buck
Made frog gigs, thrashed Mackling Spring into a suds.

("I say, dear boys! Be good. Take care.
But learn a little evil! if you dare. . . .")
His thirst once drunk, turned drunken,

And Buck Duke tossed all night, all day,
Made rusty speeches on old swapping knives,
Called names that paled the sallow-boned herbwives,
Tore off the sleeping clothes, his bed's, his own,
And never seemed to wake.
His boyish modesty ran dry,
At last the hands cooled, then the face.
Mamma stood at his bedside.
She overlooked him with a sprightly brow
Inspired by that gay mistress of mad poesy
Her elocution teacher, Miss Hattie Yow.
    "'Stop stop, pretty waters' cried Mary one day
    'My vessel, my flowers you carry away.'"

Mamma made a wreath of all her flowers:
The histrionic garden did not bear
One saucy pose when she put down the scissors;
The battered bees hung stupid in mid-air.
She worked on knees and elbows on the back porch,
That savage zinnia ornament compiled,
Then all at once cooped up her face
With hands like bird's wings—
A gesture, she knew, would have made Miss Hattie smile.

Playing

In Ugly Creek they dashed their toes.
The Cyril Mabry cows arose
And water spiders stepped aside
To watch how little girls would wade;
A summer picnic well delayed
Might miss the churn-turned fireside.

Those old folks always have been old . . .
Those childhoods tell-re-over-told
Are just a pocket full of seeds
That never generated weeds. . . .

When the little girls returned to the bank
Their little fingers swelled and shrank!
A frigid, leafless shadow lay
Upon the water-throated day.
They piled their hands to play a game—
Pretense had always been their aim. . . .
What was it, little girls became?
Take it off, knock it off, or
Have the crows peck it off—?
The little hands . . . they somehow shake;
The little bones they somehow quake.

Where's my share? Cat got it.
Where's cat? In the woods.
Where's woods? Water squenched.
Where's ox? Rope lynched.
Where's rope? "Dead and buried
Behind the new church door
And the first that laughs or grins or shows
His teeth
Gets a slap, and a kick, and a knock, and a—
Wreath."

The female bitter black tongues hum
The palms forsake the stiffened thumb
(The waiting womb! The waiting tomb—
The empty antique sitting room!)
Before the final griefs succumb—

ROBERT, YOU LEFT OUT SOME!
You left out some!
You left out some!
Watt . . . left out some . . .

Wind

From the moment Gabriella died
At an exhausted, nightless morning time
A knifestruck disattendance cast a gloom
In any place she might have chanced to be,
Even in places properly mine—
In my bedroom, at my fireside—
That made me rise at once and leave a room
Instantly her formal blank came in to me;
The one last-minute, dry-pen silence drew
A grave, regretful, canceling line through
All my blotted teas. There was nothing to say
And it was no use looking for anything,
In the cupboards, or out the door.
Long ago, something had eaten out my marrow,
And I was hungry now, for years before.

    My flaxseed-meal aunts touched my arm:
    "Faith holds no room for such alarm—"
But the wind of a suddenly-turned season,
Hard, and raw enough to move a solid shadow,
Began in flaws to rush the outer closures
And wheedle through the inner apertures,
Calling together broken flowered cups,
Uncommunicative inked-out reasons,
Recalling losses that had hinged
On cheese toast and the cats' piece-meals;
I even felt my cradle agonies
Alone, in the dark back room, revealed
In the wind fighting the oaks, seizing life
Just so. In the wind's seizure I saw her
Trudging barefoot and mudfouled
Over the clay with strength grown bodywise,
And wherever the dreamy, cultivated
Part of her had fled to—
It was not in her ghost, nervous, human eyes
I kept seeing.
                Gabriella, howl!

Sister

And we two alone here in this peace pan
Are ever strolling uphill to the old-house-place;
The path washed out, grown up, but not erased:
The wars of marriage and the family burst around us.

When I was young, folks thought me pretty.
I took my charms up to the city. . . .
I didn't like it there.
    Oh, the poems Mamma burned in those days!
You made Mamma cry. Her tears fell in the dough . . .
I'm not well, that's why. I told you so.
Why did you go and have me? I hate you all.
    Lord, help me to be more humble in this world.
(Don't tell on me. I hid the pieces in the dungeon.)
    Lord, help me to be more humble in this world!
    In that Great, Getting-up Morning, there will be another
        song!

In the old-house there was cotton,
Piled shoulder high to climb on.
Soundless and seedy—exotic,
And the floor smelled seasonround of guano.
We walked about and about the house at night.
Hear the frogs creak in the pasture! (I thought
The stars made that noise when they came out)
No! no! no! no! my dear!

Then we discovered within the close
Our exotic properties, our pretty price.
The garden radish lies on ice, the radish rose.
Smorgasbord! And the 'Venerable
Silver-throated horn' unsounded;
Dinner on the grounds! and the blessing still unsaid;
The sun that baked our mud-bread

Hides slyly in the trees
Between Spring Garden and Milton Streets
And howls at what we eat.

And riding the trolley homeward this afternoon
With the errands in my lap
I would have disfestooned my world—
A husband, more or less!
A family, more or less!—
To have alighted to a cup of kettle-tea
And someone
To whom I could lie merrily,
Use malapropisms, be out-of-taste,
Without regretting that old warfare waste,
Without acknowledging the sib discard—
Black king, black jack, black heart;
We'd play it solitary while the dusks rushed by,
More than one-flesh-and-blood,
Almost one I.

Goodbye Family

The sounds I hear from the evening chambers
    Stanch my breath.
Whether I sit alone in the parlor
    Or whether
Ladies crack nuts and ice cubes there, I hear
    Tiptoeing,
A banging head, and breath stops for fear
    Of what I am doing there
Changing and pacing in the rooms
    Of next year.
For hate-you paralyzed my lover's shrug;
    My stare
Froze down the only warmth another had,
    All her own;
Each year I dug and moved the peonies
    Longing to flare
Fat and chemically by the well-slab,
    Ingrown.
Every day I opened the drawer and
    Scanned the knives;
Were there enough, sharp enough,
    For all lives?

The years to climb! The walls to catch at!
    To cut free
And drop through the cloak closet and cellar
    Is better—
Under the foundations of God's world
    Lilily
Swimming on my side, with ear on shoulder,
    Eyes unlettered,
And intellectuality an asterisk
    Now blurred—
It's no use God's whistling, "Come back, Fido,
    Come back,

I won't tease any more." I'm in the glade
    Remembering
I meant to tell my daughter, "I looked for
    You a cattail
But they were all silked out"—
    And now the water
Meeting me around the curve, roaring, blanks
    Out all but ear:
        Not in the day time, not in the dark time
        Will my voice cut and my poison puff
        My treasures of flesh
        My gems of flashing translucent spirit,
        Nor my caress shatter them.

The Chain Gang Guard

The pick strikes differently on the rock
And some resists and some dislodges.
The cars that pass us eye us curiously—
Stodged with our eyes, our frozen triggers cocked.
They move free enough; for them, they're jolly—
The blond one, swinging, sings, "Just like a tree,
Just like a tree, planted by the waters,
I shall not be moved." Easy to see
His spirit's not yet broken. That first chow—
Nose took a squint and stomach shut its eyes;
"I can't eat that," he said. The others spat.
"You may think you can't, but, brother, you lie!"

I don't dare glance to hail the folks I know.
He'll curse or laugh or both as he sees fit,
Cry out to give a stranger's ears a whack,
And throw his hat up for a powdered nose,
Baby oh baby oh baby her,
Die to know where she's off-to up the road.
Playmate, you aint going nowheres
Unless you want to hear my gun unload.

If I had ever learned to tear-up-jack,
Got drunk enough to leave myself behind,
Could know which time to take and which to pay—
Here I stand! loaded gun across me—
As if I'd get away!

Night

I spent the night in Chastelton.
The splitting damasks hung in belts;
Those faded colors we admired
Forgot themselves in gray.
Light spider-bagged the baseboards, tired.
I climbed up to the children's room.
I knew the way.
Up steps and past a blistered stile
Along that thick oak balustrade
(You like old things? Behold!)

The carved door hung ajar.
I pushed it wide.
The birds flew from their roosts
And disappeared like mice into the sky.
Below, the garden that one time
Held itself clipped urns, hens, cones,
Of evergreen, had turned
A calendar of wastes,
A zodiac of despairs.
There was somebody there.

It was you.
You were a mortal sheen
Flickering from the negative.
You were younger than last year,
Younger than the day we were married,
Younger than the day we met.
What are you doing?
To whom are you smiling?
Where are you going?
Will you not answer me?
Answer! Answer!

Woman as Artist

I'm mother.
I hunt alone.
There is no bone
Too dry for me, mother,
Or too extra.

Have a care, boy.
The neat pearls nibbling at the chowder
Gently, with joy,
Contain powder.

> An emigrant from the mother tongue
> To say-so in the silent one,
> For me the stepped-for step sinks,
> The expected light winks
> Out; dear self, do not think
> On the ominous appetite rising insistently
> In the hour of no food. . . .
> Do not think of mice in the clock
> When you start up in your sleeping hood.
> The light feathers of a year,
> Too fine to make a pillow,
> Not fine enough to wear
> Out anywhere, drop but like milk
> Into the snow
> Of what I say and bear.

Kneel, fathers.
If my babies are right,
It is not because of you!
Or me.
But I lick them dearly,
Scrutinize their toilette,
Every tendril pleasing
On account of me. . . .

Next year I'll dig them up
And separate them.
They'll multiply
    Multiply
        Multiply
Till round the earth's ringed with Babel trumpets,
Some dark, some light,
Some streakèdy.

When I first gave the question life,
The howling naked question life,
Did I not have some inkling of the answer,
And the answer answered.
The door that closed across the room
As my door opened?

    In the morning, early,
    Birds flew over the stable,
    The morning glories ringed the flapping corn
    With Saturn faces for the surly light,
    And stars hung on the elder night.

    But in the afternoon
    Clouds came
    Cyclonic gusts and chilling rain
    Banged-to the windows of our heroine
    Beginning to chronicle her wound-up skein.
    Rib, spin.

Song

Oh my dearie,
Our childhoods are histories,
Buckets at the bottom of the well,
And hard to tell
Whether they will hold water or no.
Did Pa die before we were married?
No, he died in twenty-seven,
But I remember the wedding
Reminded me of the funeral—
When grandbabies ask,
Little do they care,
I will tell them about the man I found
That day at my plowing in the low-grounds
Lying at the edge of the water.
His face had bathed five nights.
A dark man, a foreigner, like.
They never found his kin to tell. . . .
Buckets, buckets at the bottom of the well.
It was in the paper with my name.
I found him.
I have the clipping tells all about it,
If your Grandma aint thrown it out.

Oh my dearie
When our faces are swol up
We will look strange to them.
Nobody, looking out the door
Will think to call us in.
They'll snap their fingers trying
To recollect our names.
Five nights, five bones, five buckets—
Who'll ever hear a sound?
Oh my dearie
The rope broke
The bucket bobs round
Oh my dearie

My Grandmother's Virginhood, 1879

When I disrobed to go to bed
It seemed to me like something said:
Hold your shimmy round you tight—
Somebody may be around tonight—
Aint no curtain, aint no shade—
Don't hurt none to be afraid—
    Little David McSwain!

Walked us both home from the dance
Wearing new black homespun pants.
When we got up to the door
Catched us both around the waist
And—kissed us! Lor!
What's he getting—kisses! from us for?
    Little David McSwain!

Motherhood, 1880

When Dave got up and struck a light
We'd neither of us slept all night.
We kept the fire and watched by May,
Sick for fear she might
Go off like little Tom. . . . They say
"Don't fret . . . another on the way. . . ."
They know I favor this least child.

No use to cry. But while
I made a fire in the kitchen stove
I heard a pesky mourning dove.
Lor! What's he calling "O-love" for?

Family Bible

1. UNCLE

Typical of the presents
Grandma gave Grandpa
Was Uncle Mun,
A baroque buckle
Not to be undone.
He thought before he spoke,
Abstained from drink, snuff, smoke,
Marriage; ate and dressed frugally,
Reproved respectfully
His mother's yen
For jet beads on her birthday.
Was it not thoughtful of him
On her busy death day
As she counted quilt-blocks
To elicit this data
In Spencerian pencil
Laid away in the clock
For me,
Posterity?
    My full name is Aminta Dunlap Watkins Ross.
    My mother was Merina Wilkerson.
    My father was Arnold Watkins—he carpentered—
    I married your pa Whitson Ross
    My wedding presents were a feather bed and two hens.

2. GRANDMOTHER

The hens gone on the honeymooning coach,
Squawking and scratching the black hope chest;
She made her bed and it was hard, for rest
Too hard; when broken dreams and sleep encroached
Upon stark wakefulness, she walked the stars;
Her unread eye imagined what they meant:

Job's Coffin and the Seven Sisters, the fine-print
Groups; then what said those blazing sky-far
A sky not like a page, a script not like a word,
But taking or leaving a star,
A world, as it just chose?
How the hymn book puzzled her,
Singing "Jesus and Shall"—
And the notes of the music,
If one read, like the choir!
'Tis midnight in my soul till He
Bright morning Star! bid darkness flee.

3. GRANDFATHER

The fear of hell was all,
His children wheezed,
That wore Whit Ross's pants
Out at the knees.
His poverty enraged him
(A hoe
To cultivate flint rocks,
Breeches to thwart the briers)
His wits fanned up his ignorance
Like a fire.
Something savage in him
Fought civility.
If he had but been born nobility!
Beaten sexless lifeless
Souls touched him.
When a black boy Joe died—
What had he ever had
From life to give to death?
He found a far-off part
Of meadow land
To cry his tears.
"A Christian spirit needs

Not cherry bounce,
Mint, be a good woman—
The Bible says!"

4. GRANDPARENTS

The Bible says!
The Bible looked not right to her.
It should be short, straight rules,
Not run-on continuities the stops left out
So hard to read for true.
The Bible says!
She wept before the finger.
She sought out her eldest son
In the middle of the day.
"Boy, pray for me."
His coattails, her calico black skirts
Puddled about the shoes and knees.
Was it forgiven? It was gone.
The heathen dancing
With her giggling sisters;
They flew about the room
In seedstitch weskits
Like eight wax dolls gone flaskwards.
Those were gay days!
She sighed a mournful tune
Waddling about her everyday
Affairs of life and death
(Affairs of painful life, uncertain death):
"Wild loneliness that beats
Its wings on life," she sang.
She thwacked a pone in two,
Her big hand for a knife.
Thar! stirring it severely,
And thar! into the oven . . .
Twould be wormwood and ashes.

A spray of peacock feathers
Begged from her father's house
Splattered the dining room wall.
(She pretended to Whit
That she dusted with it.)
The table was small for nine;
The honeycomb, buttered,
Hived in glass vines.

5. GRANDDAUGHTER

When she was old, deaf, widowed, my grandmother,
She came to spend a lonely night at home.
When I went to call her in to breakfast
She did not hear my brave voice for her comb
Running through her hair in little flights—
(Long, long hair as much gold as white,
Flying with old-fashioned electricity
From the comb's old-fashioned friction)
And as she rocked, her shell-combs on her knee,
Suddenly aware, she looked up at me
Through her shimmering hair, startled, and smiled.
Air ye awake, little gal?
Perhaps she thought I was admiring her.
She gave a proud, delighted, sidewise smile
Flashing her small gray teeth and elf-arched eyes,
For a ninety-eight-point-six degrees' response.
But she was disappointed, though I smiled.
Her silent island threatened me enchantment;
The joints too lithe to creak when I bent over
Sailed off without retrieving for her
A big bone hairpin wrecked upon the floor.

The day she was buried
I played sick and lay abed
Claiming fever.
I did not see her dead.

But eight months before
At Rehobath Church
On Homecoming Day
I stood with a crowd
Of boys and girls, and
Watched her cross the churchyard
Slowly, alone; from end to end
She crossed the yard,
Her head thrown back,
Swathed deep in black—
Long skirts, pointed black toes,
The wind parting her many veils,
The blue eyes beneath roving, veiled—
And leaning on a stick.
She seemed a giant Figure,
All eyes upon her;
Yet none spoke.
And all my heart said,
Run to her! Claim her!
(Wild loneliness that
Beats its wings on death)
Then the spell broke.
We who had waved across so many chasms
No longer had to say we were not close.
Was closeness more than painful separateness?
We were a constellation of detached, like, ghosts.

Welcome Eumenides

(1972)

After Twenty Years

After twenty years in France
Do you dream in French, my son? . . .
Home . . . ça existe encore.
Still, still exists Flagg Bros. store,
With new glass front, but behind
The dilapidated sheds
And packed road lined with maypops
Where you talked to the white horse.

Gloved, hatted, I kneel here
Where you by the sky-blue windows
Sang "Onward Christian Soldiers."
For I have needed pardon
Since the morning we found Dad
In the garage (It is hard
To be a father without
A son). I screamed, and without
A son to be a widow.
Shall I pray your pardon too?
Prince of Peace, absolve all warriors,
My warrior of the bow and arrow.
Your old girl married money.
She's grown stout. (*He* has ulcers.)

Last year they were in Nice
Not Normandy. . . .
My glove's rouge, with lipstick
Or with teeth. . . . Curse *men,* curse *free*—
God vault your freedom!

Oh the acres of undistinguished
Crosses make me sick.
Mother could mark Papa's grave
In the churchyard a mile from home,
By its firs and shaft. . . .

Your nothing grave . . .
                         Shame!
God I am of little understanding. . . .
But with God all things are possible. . . .
Give my son another life—
A Norwood ugliness, a bourgeois rot,
Dust and concrete, Falcons and Mustangs, not . . .

Welcome Eumenides

God called me in the morning and asked
me would I do good for Him, for Him
alone without the reputation.
                                    F.N., March 7, 1850

Who calls?
Speak, for thy servant heareth. . . .

Is it the wards at Scutari?
Or the corridors at Waverly,
Where last night eighty slept.
Our masks—my pink gown with black lace—
Moving, at five, exhilarated,
Weary from dancing, up the famous stairs. . . .

Mother! Nurse! water! . . .
I come!

But now at five they have not slept
Except the men, heads blanketed, who crept
To timeless shadow.
Two thousand deathbeds that one winter.
Last May my window gave
On a thousand Turkish flowers,
Two thousand English graves.
Two thousand deathbeds that one winter—
Who thinks of that now?

Who calls?
Not my child
(*O God no more love*
No more marriage)
Only my British Army.

(*Dear Aunt Mai, kiss all babies for me.*)
Oh my poor men I am a bad mother

To come home and leave you to your Crimean graves.
73 percent in 8 regiments in 6 months
From disease alone. (Who thinks of that now?)

There was a white rose in the New Garden cloister.
(The idol of the man I adored)
Richard, the sea breaks against the sea wall.
("You could undertake that,
When you could not undertake me.")
The plough goes over the soul.
    My Hilary ateliered,
    Femme espaliered, or, woman staked.
    The apricot bears against the south wall
    Daughters too basked at hearth.
    (No more love, no more marriage!)
Which of the chosen ever chose her state?
To hide in love!
Lord, seek Thy servant elsewhere. . . .
    Yet He calls.

I was not invited.
At home at Embly, Wilton, Waverly,
I, sated with invitations,
I, presented to the poor Queen,
I, worthy of the Deaconesses of Kaiserswerth,
Asked by the birthday child to every fête,

I was unwelcome.
The others came.
Two hundred by the shipload,
Jolted from stretchers,
Feverishly crawling up the hill
Through the ice-needled puddles.

I guarded the anteroom
Holding my nurses back, immune

To the cries, the sudden retching spasms, the all
But visible odors. (*Abandon hope all ye who enter here.*)
The mold grew on the walls.

    Blessed are the merciful,
    Says my crowned cross.

Pails of arrowroot, some port . . .
And then, all Balaclava broke loose.
Quick now, old sheets (the dying wait)
Speed, needle! This is no hooped French knot;
A deathbed is required.
    (Where did I yawn
    In the face of the gilt clock
    Defying it to reach 10?)
    Stuff straw for deathbeds, for deathbeds,
    For deathbeds.
    Not one shall die alone.
    I die with each.
    Now hurry to the next lax hand, loose tongue,
    Quick messages for forever.
    Mr. Osborne knelt down for dictation.
    His pencil skirmished among lice.
    At last, the chance for a rich and true life.

Outside, the wind rises.
    Wood! the fire dies. . . .
        There is no wood.
    The operating table then. Yes, chop it up.
        (For the operation Mr. Osborne
        Held up the patient with his arms and knee.)

Pen—paper—*vite!*
They demand supplies . . .
Ah ohhh the engine in my head. . . .
Claret and white flour for the Persian adventurer!
    Must I repeat:

Do not
    attach to the cutlets
    (1) rags (2) nails (3) buttons
    . . . surgical scissors

. . . that you can join me on the twenty-seventh
(Crème Harlequin aux Meringues—or dariolettes?)

And again. Please keep:
    a. Toilets covered.
    b. Windows open.
Orderlies: Eat not the rations of those men asleep.
    (*The éclat of this adventure of mine!*)

I dreamed . . .
Compulsive dreaming of the victim.
The rich play in God's garden.
Can they be forgiven?
Their errors gambol scintillating
Under the chandeliers like razors honed.
I murder their heaven,
I, starving, desperate, diseased. . . .
    ("You'll catch something and bring it home.")
Mother, you were willing enough
To part with me to marriage.
No, I must take some things;
They will not be given.
I dream.
    Saints are non-conformists,
    Ladies gone into service,
    Serving ladies with one talent;
    Cast ye the unprofitable servant into outer darkness.

Still-room, pantry, linen room.
Green lists, brown lists, red lists.
Come to me, yearbk of statistics
Of the Deaconesses of Kaiserswerth,

My love, my escape,
My share.
I dreamed of you; now I dream on you:
A hundred baby prayers;
All days garlanded with birthdays, prayers and flowers,
Rye tea. Elevenses: broth without bread:
At last, the chance for a rich and true life.

A girl, desperately fortified in my castle,
The starched pure linen,
Scalded plates, the sanitary air,
The facile word killed soul-ferment.
Six courses starved the spirit.
 And I said of laughter, mad,
 And of mirth, what is it doing?
I dreamed of all things at man's mercy.

Another boy reached for my hand.

Nurse, keep away. I'm filthy.
My own mother could not touch me.
And I looked sharply down. I was *not*
Wearing my great Paree panjandrum of black velvet.
It was my shawl, my pockets.
 (It is not lady's work.)
I got the burned wing ready
For eight hundred, sheets and warm food.
"I think I am in heaven," one soldier said.

 Bridget looked up. A lady in black
 Walked up the Lea Hurst drive.
 Miss Flo! Our little beauty—
 Come home to die?
 Or come home dead.
 I have looked on Hell.

I wear black for you O British Army.

At night they flare in this soft room:
The long flickering wards,
The muddy uniforms, and sullied faces,
The black, dried, inky blood.
I can never forget.
I stand at the altar of the murdered men
And while I live I fight their cause.

Which of the chosen ever chose her state?
I who looked for some small stanch
Found the world's blood,
Armed with my handkerchief.
Armed with statistics:
Halt! wagons of the heavy artillery.
Cease and desist, wheels of the War Office.
  ("She wept very much.")
I survive them all.
I am sure I did not mean to . . .
No one ever did give up so much to live
Who longed so much to die.
Venez me consoler de n'être pas morte. . . .

. . . Much obliged, Dear George
For your Latin Hey Diddle Diddle
(O God no more love no more marriage.)

Ni lire, ni écrire, ni réfléchir.
I wear black for you O British Army.

  Another boy reached for my hand. . . .

Sir George, thank you
For the Greek Humpty Dumpty.
  (Still He calls.)
Venez me consoler de n'être pas morte.
Venez chez moi on Harley Street.
Bordure de jambon á la Sauvaroff—
Or . . . quenelles de veauf á la Villeroi?

—The pungent meat pots at Scutari
Seasoned with iron pins, bolts, rusty nails
Tied to each packet.
A skinned sheep lay in the ward all night
To tempt our appetites.
The backed-up drains,
The floor inch-deep in sewage
Seeping under the door.
A thousand diarrheas vs. twenty chamber pots.
Ma'am, I've gone here.

Entry: March 10, 1866. *O!*

    I who could not live
    Without silence and solitude
    Harassed by Parthe's crewel Jesse tree . . .
    (Mother *lied* about the money). . . .
They left my owl locked in the empty house.
In my torment come dreams,
Dreams of Athena who left the Parthenon
To keep house in my pocket,
Forsaken in her feathers,
Her head winding and unwinding,
Eyes blank of me. . . .
Eyes at Scutari following
From cot, from floor, from table, winding-sheet.
For all things at our mercy
Give us grace.

To a Young Writer

If you like love and fame
Shop early, get your shots
Don't spit, and pass with care—
Avoid at all costs
Death, breakdown, despair;
They'll fall on you,
Flock-peck to pieces wounded mouse:
I always thought so—
You know he lacked the drive
It had to come—
Dear friends consign you
To sanatorium, prison, and the pall.
No, keep your chair,
Tuck your wits in,
Say finally
I did outdure them all

The Young Writer's Reply

But, sir, you know I saw the cops
Remove you from that Bleecker garbage can
Agog with pot.
Remember—analyzing Donne's Sermons
On your Payne Whitney cot?
(Your comments were brilliant, brilliant—
As noted in my journal on the spot.)
All of us heard you rake your wife
For coolness to your whore.
    We wrote it down.
        Laurel becomes a devastated brow.

Courtesy Call, 1967

I'm back.

But you sleep now,
Who used to be the guardian of the stream.
It needs no guarding now; it's dreaming, too—
Narrower, deeper, sluggish, frosted with leaves.
I think it's comatose.
One used to see, a mile away, wind whip
Your leaves to wrongsideout to sun.
A wind could hardly find this glen today.
That hill was open pasture!
Just now I had to fight my way
To find a spot pine trunks
Were not too logjammed to squeeze through.
It was hard even to find you.
I thought I knew so well.
When the boys dug the swimming hole
They turned the stream;
But it's gone back now,
Their pool washed in,
Their turn filled in with trees—
Trees old (but younger
For trees than they are for boys). . . .

Except that you've grown truly ancient . . .
I? The same.
The same, and elderly.
Like you trapped in some far neglect;
Reflections deepened, dulled,
Our voices out.

Flight

She could not understand it.
By chance twice that day
　turning her head in backward glance,
　she glimpsed a bird perched on her shoulder.

That night, a cry—a devil's squeal,
　a beating at the upstairs window ledge,
　a clawing at the screen in crazed appeal.
Then in the moonlight, wings
　dizzied the eye angling across
　the bed, window to window,
　whirling frantically, and were lost.

　　　　—John, a bird got in our room last night,
　　　　—Oh, Lucy! . . .
　　　　　　But *A spirit escaped,* she thought,
　　　　　　And dreaded news.

Next week, two green flies
　fought at the attic window—
Something not freed—
　ensnared in its own flight. . . .
And a letter telling
　of a certain night—
　an old friend met at the airport
　by wife, psychiatrist,
　and plainclothesman. . . .
　"Our genius is doing well."

Epitaph

She lies where doves call, bedded,
From the creek bank; creek bedded, too,
Willow and gum ruched honeysuckle;
The Saint graveyard's neglected.

Her house was screenless; doors stood wide;
Leaves drifted unwatched down the hall;
Hens left warm eggs indoors.
A stray lamb maddened by the scolding floor
Galloping broom to bed to wall to wall
Fell out the back door finally, prayers-answered.

For she was always in the low-grounds
Chopping cotton, or by the orchard
Binding wheat with wheat-strands,
Thinning the corn slips in the new-ground field,
Then home to snatch the coffee pot
Up off the floor (where the baby'd played),
Lay table, before they all got in.

—Kate, this brew's not fit to drink.
   —What? . . .
            Oh Lord.
—Don't cry, Kate
   —But I can't help it
   I never cried for shirtwaists
   Or china cups
   Or crocheted pillow shams. I've not.
   But oh to have it said of me
   She boiled the gosling in the coffee pot . . .
      Poor gosling!

FROM
New and Selected Poems
(1983)

The Painted Bridge

It didn't seem like history. Seemed, more,
expediency. . . .

I'm walking to the beauty shop. On Rugby Road
a fractured fume of sodden leaf
and Phi Delts' pizza lunch, and through the pane
one of their rout white-coated, hands behind,
waits unattending in the wings, waits out
the weary midday to the coming night.

With harness creak of shoulder bag
I mount the railroad bridge, its college news
furled to the wall: day-in-and-day-out cries
in sky blue headlines on pea green BLANK DUKE;
blood red on U-Haul orange overnight
CONGRATS TO SHIRLEY MARILYN
ON PREMIERE OPENING.

        A starchy stroke
whitewashes smut, then BE HEALTHY LOVE A NURSE
A PHI-NOMINAL YEAR AT U-V-A
and JJ as a bare rug (pink on gray).
I null it out.

A tomtom pulsing shakes the maple heads:
below me down the track the train comes on
its big light blazing midday head-on course.
I've never in my life till now crossed when
a train was passing.

        A striped-capped head
leans out the cab, and arm thrown all-out up
waves wildly.
—Never seen a woman cross a bridge before?—

His eager face ignites at happenstance, but
I hang fire.

        And suffocating fumes
engulf the wavy birthday caps,
his carpe diem's capped by captioned bridge—
he's under.

        I descend the railroad street.

Below the bridge the blue-lined buckets and
caked lids, the wares the news was made of,
litter the ditch's glittering careless depth.

I'm off. Off for my—*set.*

The Going Away of Young People

September 1, 1975

1

This was the day
The crumbs from last night's dinner
Lay all day on the table.

Your room filled only by sunlight
Is darkened by the late sleeper.

> You forgot your love.
> I'd mail it but
> There's the chore of string
> And paper and
The timbre of hi-fi turned off
Strings of the psyche.

> Anyway it's stuff I'm used
> To stumbling over in various
> Recesses of my house
> Wondering why I haven't
> Given it away, put it
> To some use—
> But keep on hoarding it, ashamed.

2

And our sailers-away hang yet full sail
In our autumn windows
The windows across the street
Becalmed of young people.
Grass infiltrates their marigolds.
The garage cries out.

3

I won't say good-bye
But all leave-taking is permanence.
We can't be sewed back up.
My mother's face at the window
Like a postage stamp
Hinges a faded September.

4

Windows between Septembers
More and more windows
Muffling, fogging over,
At last reflect only me
In car windows, kitchen windows,
Across-the-street-windows
This window I open over your bed
In case you should come back
For what we both forgot.

Women's Terminal Ward

she was walking the two white Spitzes
in the dusk of College Circle

                                       three wraiths
    dreaming absently of that female babe
    the chairman forbade that she adopt

she was waltzing into class late

                            wobbling
under a giant amaryllis urn
rotating it on the desk   egging it on
lost in its angles
                 where to turn?

shelled with cancer
    faded hair sheeting the bellied
pillow   in the veiled ward she wakes
    to her old students
                    glows
   cherubic
go long! you girls oughtn't be kissing me
    we kiss her again
I have reaped where I have not sowed. . . .
    (night nurse running her soft legs off elsewhere)
we linger still
            grayly
   amaryllis
a little woozy   *the bedpan please*
    the white duck shirttail   the lifting hard
and the balding vulva   the shell of daughters
   looms in this fleeing light
this manless ward

New Dust

Who was Athena's pet—
Be glad you're dead.
That you should see the shadow fleshen!
The shade caught in the arachnid net—

> *This dust was Randall and they say*
> *That almost on his lucky day*
> *He found his only luck to be*
> *The dark concrete of 53*

But I'm Athena's pet. . . .
Send me my jeweled bridle,
My Austrian sweater and more books. . . .
    Shaking off rejected Anteia
    I soared again
    Freed of that heaviness.
    I watched her fall into the human stars.
    What gods would take her part?
    She said they did.
    I wander in the Plain of Wandering
    In October, in full light of Pegasus
    Having repulsed the lady's love,
    Black men in blackness.

(My hoofs strike sparks from you—
I collect them in a basket
For my daughter.
    Empty the shelves!
I flew my library to Baltimore
And ate it.)

TO THE 15 BYPASS. . . .
    To be fifteen!
    Sabertooth at the Joint Library,
    Gnawing Fannie's knee. . . .
    Here by the laboring highway

With painful hands I strain . . .
With a bottle, but no spoon . . .
—"Let *that* be a medicine to you."
(I tell you it sure helps
to have some sympathy).

I draw towards HWY. 29.
Cars pass— to—
To Greensboro— that's home—
Lucy— and supper. . . .
     A cruel cold snap.
     Not a blackberry winter—
     Winter! and a white beard.
     Lost, those vernal altitudes,
     Clambering
     Past my last equinox.
     There was a time, I drove.
     (For the sin of surpassing
     They turned on him—
     The gods, the mount he rode.)

          But what if the story had been different?

Mother said I had her eyes.
What I'd give for my own! . . .

This dread is too dreadful

A car has two eyes
A windshield two faces

     For me, one unflowering autumn
     It went so ill that I

Two heads two headlights CAR

     Oh mother
     I've broken one of my immortal bones
     blind
     my immortal I

When Robins Return

When I see robins running in the grass
I wonder which he is, and if at last
he's as he wished, a robin in next life,
a shed eccentric, a wing-risen brass.

I wonder when I hear at dawn in May
that volubility at serious play
whether it's born verbal charm to tempt
earthworms, his Methodist constraint to pray,

or just a brisk happy advice to nests,
tutelage of the cuss and discuss
style, that taught more than we'd meant to learn,
from one who lived here wifeless and childless.

I see him flying with his lady mother
south, falls, to the Gulf. They doff their feathers
(at last she thinks him lyrical and bold)
evenings under magnolia weather,

play two-hand bridge, shuffling the red and black
cards with goldish talons. The fatal pack
is marked a different way this go-around:
justly, he'll eat her while she's fighting back.

Va. Sun. A.M. Dec. '73

morning mtns &

                    interstitial deer

sheets flick

wedding ring clicks

                    against the headboard

things are disappearing forever

    mtns. behind the mounting pines

    deer shot

    wedding rings flung in drawers

    Suns. no diff from rest of the wk.

    Va. no diff rest of the world

In dead-land nothing changes.

Limits

Only he
Remembered the day we met
And only I
The day we said goodbye:
"Last day of June, our first blackberry pie,"
He always said.
A wood fire in the summer kitchen,
The hottest day. . . . A squall in the bedroom.
    I can't remember.

Nor he,
The December cube of clay,
The storm the day before,
How the bare trees
Played Giant Step in the dawn wind,
Or how
On the other bed, rhythmically
Touching her knuckles to the wall,
My mother slipped forever into fantasy.

Only he
Remembered the spoken hate
(Its change too sheepish to impart)
Saw daggers still growing
In bristling clump out of my heart.

I beg you, kids—no memorials, please.
Don't write poems to me. Don't bother.
What we said we said. What's unsaid lacks ears.
In this I'm like my father.

To Future Eleanors

How will you
cut off from Zions,
    fall on your knees among the lions?
What if you
cut off from hymns
    confound worksong with anthem

Cut off from Scripture
    find sense suspect
    and worship
        incoherence—
        distrust the laces
        and adore the tangled thread?

        What of you
    without a holy thing,
    but every sacrilege
    of the sacrileged class?

Godsave your unsuspecting fists
grasping the fiery ladder bare,
your forehead
fighting a wordless solitaire.

Without some future language
how can I ask you?
If I could ask in Euphorese,
Moonskrit, in Ecolow. . . .

    What will you do with
    Grandma's savings—
    those relics atticked
    in your head
    of effort, vision?

On pain of death, scratch pictures
in the dust
          as she did—
I fear my after-thirst.

New Girls

Devious, devious are
primroses in shade
collecting sunshine
without sunshine.
Sprawling on the grass
they grip their books.
The strings of summer
ring without answer.
Hello Juliana?
Hello Augusta?
What are you doing tomorrow?
Sleeping,
            sleeping.

Numerous the shades
under primroses,
shifting sands and
sets and seasons,
reaching for the
fellow pillow,
reaching for the
strings of summer,
too treble, too shining
for inside eyes.

The Ribbon to Norwood

January 5, 1971

Will all be well?
    To outfly the snow.

Waking in the dark . . . I think
    he kneels at the hearth,
    radiates the ceiling. . . .
    No. Older than that. Old.
    My father lights no fires;
    I expect no hearth.
But today I go,
my day there a dream
in her deep drowse.

As the stars shine all day,
the stoplight wanes
all night in the void: I go
to the place no eye is on,
to see-after the day stars
the stop and go
the house and bed
the screen unhooked
by a blind hand
dying to clasp mine.
Is it mine? Am I the one she knows?

The bus rides high.
Frozen fog blobs the coves,
crawls, blobs, up the streams . . .
to curse me with unknowing.
    Will all be well?
Flood wreckage lies,
crossed branches like
wishbones in the snow.

My wish keeps her alive. . . .
(He died.
I neglected the vigilance
of my wish. He died.)
One bedroom shoe . . .
(In my blind anger
sunning the stained mattress
I did not see the wasps that stung,
late winter wasps, their hour come.)

Snow ending, rain ending, fog lifting—
Groping along the ribbon—
Ariadne be with me now.

A smell of sleep on the rattling bus.
Morning breaking,
morning twilight, oatmeal twilight.
A lighter snaps. . . .
    Light deepened—a blinding crack above—
    Jule reared—and they raced home
    Jule stepping high, he scurrying
    to hold the plow above the grass. . . .
I jump.
A red-brick genie
whirls up unbottled on the window.
Gone.
She "saw" him:
"The moon and stars hung on his face."
Can the past be wrested
from oblivion by a wish?

    With one purpose only—
    to outfly the snow.

Past the James,
the faucet of the Alleghenies,

silt clogged, poured toward England.
It that sees the thread of the family . . .
it that knows. . . .
From the Westminster tombs
to Jamestown churchyard. . . .
    Did she sleep all night
    drawn up
    as against a cliff,
    clinging
    to escape the rising waves,
    each wave icier
    more muscular?
    And the linnets gone.
    Dreamed of thin hammered spoons,
    the comforting street puddles of home,
    splashed silk petticoats. . . .
    Waked to the stockade,
    red faces, through red eyes.
It that spins the thread of generations, that
spatters nest eggs in the wilderness,
seeds ledges,
lands in Cedar Grove. . . .

Yonder, fog is tumbling
over peaks, is
looking for something,
going somewhere . . . home.
It has forgotten its form,
how to proceed towards what.
Back. That's the direction.
One weather vane points South,
one, England
one, infinity.
Now we skim into sky, green dawn,
forest hardedge.
Now we shall make out the sum.

The Tye brighter than the sky
is singing the day.
Now the nests can be told,
and honeysuckling over pine and creek
sings home free, home free.

Voices waking. . . . *Is it day? Mommy!*
Gobs of phlegm . . .
Seem lak everybody want
to get out of D.C.
on the week-end.

Hemerocallis green the banks,
a taint of spring in my pure winter.
    (The practical nurses get
    dollar-nour.
    If you can gettum.)
        (She keeps the windows locked.
        The chimney talks.
            Lucy: 942-5764)

Into churning fog . . .
there floats by in the drifts
two orphans:
    a broken chimney with hearth-foot;
    a broken mammoth oak:
these two left on the field.
(We are beautiful a day.)

Only this ribbon of daylight
between eternities.
            It
that spins the thread of generations. . . .

Blue Ridge retreating,
pursued by rain,
rain descending, road descending
past cedars and rail fences.

Woman advances with cane to mailbox.
    Did I remember to answer?
    Her pencil weathers the mails.
A fat-nosed pony in a field
with busy, bushy tail
has fallen from her schoolgirl drawing,
and hangs, stuffed, on that wall of sky.

    Threaders Long Grade—
We dive into kudzu,
trestle the river where
Lynchburg's villas tooth the bluff.
We make a grand entrance.
The bus is late—
but here! air brakes announce.
Three gray sisters, not going,
say goodbye to an aging niece,
their three hats,
square, round, trapezoid,
somehow intermeshed.
Niece pecks each cheerfully,
subtracts her years from theirs,
glad to be off.
Write, write! she smiles.
They do not smile.
Then, smallest-oldest bullying the keys,
they're off to car and home,
each dreaming of that roundless
squareless, trapezoidless life
of her own each is
sure she could have had.
    So ends her brave fight
    with a new world—
    in passion for the devourer.

Snow thin and thinner.
A bird up-up-up and over the flying bus.

To see where other roads go!
Not just this, leading steel-wire on.

Chatham's net of streams,
its crevices of woods
show snow beech-laced.
    Get out the crocheted tablecloth. . . .
       (some spilled boiled custard)
    Will all be well?

A gray Victorian steeple pricks the holly.
    A gale of berries,
    her dreams fruit
    by the empty house.
    They were just cuttings
    When we put them out you know. . . .
We drowse.
A cemetery gorgeous with
dozens of dead red Christmas wreaths. . . .
Celebrate the season. . . .
    I am working hard on my birthday candles.

Passengers continuing to Greensboro. . . .
    Try landing here?
    Transferring to another person?
Danville's bus station madonna
in babushka and work shoes
hands out tracts.
In the net which they hid
is their own foot taken.
And in an anguished, hurried hand
across the cross:
Micah 7

Habakkuk 1:17
As the fishes that are taken in an evil net
so are the sons of men snared in an evil time.
I think she knows my problems.

So think they all.
All hands reach for her answers.
Thank you, madonna.

> (Somebody to sleep in the house with her.
> *Note:*
> *There is a 1–3 yr. waiting list.*)

GREENSBORO 21M.

Goin Yanceyville.
Don think my mama goin live very long.
    In her voice, some-old-lonesome
    freight train whooping at the crossing.
Will this loosestrife live?
    Now hit's a wild thing,
    a wild thing used to do-without.
To make them live. To hold them back.
They pull me on.
That shadow, racing on the meadow
is more real, more permanent.
It, at least, shadow forever. But we—
Do you subscribe to that domino
theory of life—
one goes, all go?
    Next! next in line.

All that week
We had a fire in the fireplace;
the chill wraithed round the French doors,
my thoughts of her thoughts

melding into an impending thought.
That's gone.
This ribbon I prepare slacks in my hand.
She waits for me in dreams
wheeled into limbo rooms
off cut-off corridors where

she feigns a sanity
by parroting my tenderness:
    "You're my darling!"

I went back to the farm and
looked for our dog-days,
their buried bones—
Why hadn't we known
we would be coming back?
Here are the rubbed dust wallows,
the burrow coiling to the labyrinth.
Still traveling, abiding, I descend
and muse, a muse of sorts,
in my own plot.

In Case of Danger

                        I am sending my son
an emergency survival kit:
                        flares
to light up wild mountainous terrain to
searchers in planes;
                        inscrutably furled
space blanket, tested against exposure
at Everest by recent explorers;
small high-calorie ration to sustain
one really strayed to the edge of the world.
I include a candle for him to set
in a can of sand in the car. I have
read just so much heat will keep a stranded
                        motorist from freezing.

My son lives quietly, mostly browsing
in libraries in Iowa City,
lingering sometimes late at bar
amberizing Freud and Philip Levine
with his friends; occasionally he
spends a morning at the Laundromat.

        But once when four he ran headlong
        towards the edge of an unrailed deck
        in Le Havre; a ship's guard jumped in front.
        I was wearing a tissue wool suit
        and a brown hat.
                        I had to sit down.
        Again, at ten alarmed us all
        rising to chart Jupiter's moons—
        at four A.M., when a straggler
        might have entered the dark house, or
        he been molested by a milkman.
        In London when he was so ill

I watched the sea birds at sunrise flap
along the Thames beyond the obelisk,
and sick with fright by the deranged cot
prayed for this safe time.

I must write a letter of instructions:
When in Himalayas. . . .

Rachel Plummer's Dream

Winter 1836

You never shut your eyes.
You always looked.

At the grizzled scalp you somehow recognized
even without the blue eyes and mustache,
through your blood that was Like to Strangle you
lying face down, tied,
      through the mass beating.

After five days without a Mouth of Food—
days of silence—slogging—stamina—
part of the skinclad band to the high timber,
you could not but Admire the Countrey
though short of breath from fasting, burdened with
your unborn baby, tentskins on your back.

You never turned your head
      from Little Pratt's
                calling,
    drawn from you.

When the unborn, born in captivity,
let live a week or so, was made their sport,
bounced on the frozen ground till lifeless,
you held your arms for it   and somehow
breathing new life in it, fired their new rage.
    You watched it   on a rope
whirled out by braves aponyback
till shredded on the cactus,
then thrown into your lap, a tattered mass,
and buried tearless with your hands and prayers
of thanks for its release.

You breathed the Purest Are you ever breathed
those snowy summits, Admired the Timber,

66

the Fine Springs, the Snow Rabbitt, undefiled—
(your fingers scarred with dressing hides, your feet
black-bitten) counted the advances of
the antelope, their turns, noting their
diminishing proximity, ghostly escape:
mused at the buffalo grazing in
the phantom sea—it was "a sort of gas."

Bound to see, you crashed the powwow, ignored
their cuffs—a dog that *would,* spoke Indian,
heard Indian—save one white curse
a fat-mouthed Beadie sought you out to give—
ate roots Stol'n from the Mouse's Holes,
refused the serving of the roast enemy; it was a foot.

You burned to see—as for example,
the inside of those mountain caves
before decamping;
I see you all wrapped up
        dipping flax wicks
into some tallow got from buffalo—
with these your makeshift candles and firewood,
a flint—with your young mistress took the Pieded Horse
on the uprising trail.
        Inside,
she took quick fright (she smelled the water)
but you would not go back.

Again, where it got dark, you struck the light,
and the splendor blinded.
She cried out, threatening you.
You slugged her with a stick of wood, wrestled,
ready to kill her for the sight
that was to come.

By some odd chance, your light knocked to the ground
burned on. You took it up, squinted—
the cave burst into light, imperative. But first

you led her, tamed, the miles back to the mouth;
at last made your long way in that unearthly
twinkling dark, beside the crystal river,
to sound of mighty falls ahead,

                              plunging
how far?   into what unknown places?
     caught echoes of your dying baby's cries;
like tranced Ezekiel in Babylon
     descried the noise of wings, of wings let down—
though briers and thorns be with thee, not afraid!

and a Human Being came   comforting
releasing   balming   transfusing. . . .
Your captors, waiting at the mouth, half gave you up.

How analyze
     this parapsychologic episode
     this spiritual hiatus where
you closed your eyes a whole day and a night,
on through a second day?—
                              I discount sex.
So worn, half-starved, and suicidal—
     they say, consumptive, too.
The realist, you painted not at all.

I see him, see his gifts. He chose: to bathe
your wounds that never pained again,
that Resurrection flaring in the cave,
those stars in earth, time stopped
and you with eyes to see.

In the Bitter Roots

One who's never crossed the Mississippi
and never will, now—
how can I think I stand too
in the place
in Clark's stupendous mountains
escape unsure
thinking myself, too
part of a world cut off, receding?
They think me dead;
I fight, still, in this death,
these crossed meridians.
        "If we should git bewildered
        in these mountains—"

What, never to find
the River that Scoalds All the Others,
never present (the faithful buffoon) medals
to the tribes of Jefferson's red children?
to know unseen the Bitter Roots,
the Head that pained me not so much as yesterday?
to scratch my name, first vandal,
on Pomp's Pillar—

Only to stand watching
the chimneys take the sun
no sponge dry enough for the tears
no bowl adequate for the mixed feelings
only—she standing at the window
by the gulf
trapped in these mountains
trapped in this face,
bewildering decay,
like him without one prayer
one begging phrase

blown toward Virginia and native gods.
Can I think to find
a past, a past self, in these passes,
in hospital at Sevastopol,
following among Comanche squaws?
Yes, and more,
I proceed without a guide
at this stage of the expedition
though it's known madness.

Days Going/Days Coming Back

(1991)

At the Altar

That bag you packed me
when you sent me
to the universe—
camp after camp I've opened it
debating whether to unpack—
        Not yet, not yet—
Why did I feel so much in it
was dangerous on the playground,
too good for everyday,
feel those splendid fireworks
hazardous to institutions,
unmannerly to etiquette,
so that, time after time,
I found myself saying
        Not yet?

At each new place I faced it,
it suggested,
Here spread out your things,
put on this coat,
open this bottle—
        No, not yet . . .
sometimes throwing something out,
giving things away,
lightening my load. . . .

The more I pull out,
the more it seems, some days,
is left inside,
the heavier it is.

Sometimes I think this package
is almost a door
the opening of which
careening across heaven
could be fatal.

Some days now I wonder if I'll ever
dare face my given garments—
permanently wrinkled,
surely out of date—
your travel-thought
wasting in its tissue, flesh-corrupt—
till I've absorbed it,
like those stitches that dissolve
in an incision
where something's been removed.

Short Foray

A yellow jacket flew into my taxi
    stopped in traffic near the bank.
It hung between me and the driver,
    feinting indignantly,
    complaining of the small headroom
    under the stained blue plush,
    then plunged out to the pickup truck ahead
    and settled on a corner of its bed,
    an amber scab.

My driver never twitched an earring;
    he idled lassitudinously,
    one with the motor; half-dozed,
    seemed not to apprehend
    age an infirmity, imminent bee sting,
    instant allergy and death in twenty minutes.

He was no doubt half-thinking of
    the traffic buzzing both ways,
    that squad car parked beside the bank,
    my tip, his lunch, his weekend—
    sweet circumfluencies.

I had been thinking of
    the present for my granddaughter,
    gift wrapped by an expert, a contrivance
    sure to please a one-year-old,
    the salesman said—while I was hoping
    he didn't see the big spot on my dress
    (discovered on my way over)
    and so withhold the princess wrap
    from a blind old lady and unknowing baby.

Naturally one doesn't remember being one—
    what one liked then, if one knew then—

not even what one's child liked—
    was she ever one? She likes new knaveries:
    lentil pilaf, home videos.

I didn't say a word about the bee,
    or coffee stain, or what I thought.
When we moved on I lost the yellow jacket,
    lost whether he kept clinging to the truck,
    went to the bank, or soared off over us.
No clue to what he meant, rushing my taxi.
Did he know it was October, bees-up time,
    and take this warm day for a last rich look
    at the boundaries of things, a day of
    stinging a boundary or two if he felt like it,
    playing time bomb?
Did he smell wild asters somewhere in a ditch?
Or did he just ride into town on that pickup
    and mean to go home on it?

Harvest, 1925

It took two nights to shuck the Hawfields' corn,
    piled, foreskinned, altar high,
        outside the crib.
Lanternlight. Hard trolling motions.
    Dark pent-up communion,
        with supper first, many
women together, in church clothes
    preparing food relentlessly
        as if for some dread rite.
Big Helen Hawfields
    (her long sultry breasts,
        her deep unwilling laugh)
stalked the harvest table,
    lost out the window in
        the high, encroaching winter wind,
the empty calyxes
    of cotton, a spinster's net—(*o*
        do not let the world depart
nor close thine eyes against the night)—
    she filled the lanterns
        trembling, the long wicks heavy
with combustible,
    all the blurred brandy dreams
        in her outskirts
gathered in one drunk longing
    for Tattoo's broad body.
        Below the shuck pile
was a paradise
    lipped by wild plums
        in troubled tangle;
his Maggie found them there,
    stood, hard cheeked, dazed
        at Tattoo's gnashing grin—back
at the mourners' bench!—

at Helen's bent-up stuttering,
weeping, behind the plums,
a lactate field mouse,
shucks cleaving
to her teats.

Captive Voices

They always prayed at last.
If not to God, to death.

> The trees are turning again,
> bedding down for winter. . . .
> Our feather bed was getting flat;
> did she find more geese? . . .
> He went round and round on this tether.
> Then the dogs had his bones.

> > My children are preparing themselves.
> > When I was sick last year.
> > In the meantime,
> > I ride my stationary bike,
> > and stay right here near my doctor.

The chapter began so well.
It was over the hills and far
away, and the stars still out.
Even when, at daybreak,
they appeared on the path,
we were not sure—so unwarlike,
and in their language.

> My contract only stipulated
> there be no transfer,
> and there was none, per se.
> Nobody made a killing. . . .
> Some people are like dogs in money,
> don't know which way to turn,
> guess there's something in it,
> something mysterious, sniffworthy—
> eat some, drink some, bury some.

Five days later it was not
whether there will be any dinner—

the word didn't apply.
We eyed the offal thrown out to the dogs.
We eyed the dogs.
In January the braves couldn't get near game
for the noise of the snow-crust breaking;
so it was only some old fox and raccoon bones
boiled till the strings were chewable,
but I did get mine down, and life came back.

> I thought I'd die while she ate that rice pudding;
> there were just four big shrimps in my whole salad.
> But I was down to 125 Wednesday.

—or prayed to death,
i.e., to the old squaw, faced
like the Devil (where had
Squire Knight observed the Devil?)—
who took a board and shoveled
coals onto the Captain's back
after he fell at last
and lay upon his belly.
After he'd gone round and round
on the coals, tethered.
> (If only I had listened to Wawatum!
> Often that winter he had been wakened
> by *the noise of evil birds.*)
Then they scalped him.

> It's the darkness—do you hear it?
> I went and sat out in the yard.
> The moon had great big eyes. It wanted
> brush against me like a cat.
> Not especially affectionately . . .
> Pain is what hurts the most. . . .
> Then he stood up again, inside the flames.
> But I think he did not feel pain any more.

Well, the doctor didn't want me to become addicted.
So it was Tantalus all over again, with the Tylenol.
I just went wild around the house at night,
upstairs and downstairs, looking for relief.

Having no shoes against the snow
I stopped and wrapped up my feet in my blanket,
but, growing stiff, and seeing a frozen linnet
under the bushes where I sat, got onto hands and knees,
crawling, I think, several miles, as I thought, east.

    During the ice storm
    We lost power five whole days.
    Soon as they'd fix it, another limb would fall.
    People *suffered.*
    Nobody keeps a pile of blankets now;
    and hundreds of dollars lost in freezer pack,
    just when people thought they had something ahead.

They were not strong on landscape,
being captives.
Raising the eyes and looking far
requires a certain off-guard.
Requires if not pleasure in, some
concord with one's status quo.
Mountains were never sublime and
forests did not breathe grandeur;
the rising sun recharged vigilance and the stars
were reproachful for routes lost.

    We put these pines in to screen out
    their trash cans (of course in summer
    air conditioning helps drown out the mowers)
    and we bought Tim a telescope he's never used.
    Too much city light.
    Of course, we love this house.

I keep biting the skin off my lip.
I don't know what I'd be upset about
unless it's that baby yelling Mommee.
You see two people were needed:
somebody to take Dad to the hospital
and somebody to stay with Mom.
That's why it happened—
I couldn't be two people.

Life's no longer simple.
The hunger of the first part
sues the hunger of the second part.

I carry my prayer on a stick:
Over-population is murder.

Where Somebody Died

The self refuses to appear
    in this bare place.
It fears that mute chair
    and the still window.
The sunlight scares it.
There might rise up a sound.
The door doesn't like to move,
    and the crow out there
    hesitates; he knows
    a hole flown into by mistake
    would make a bite of him.
What was sits standstill in the chair,
    hangs, stunned, against the dry-eyed light.
Nobody in sight.
Inanimate things, still lifeless.
This room's so empty
    I doubt I'm standing here;
    there can't be room for me
    and total emptiness.
Only some far-off sounds persist.
The brute truck
    over the interstate.
The flames in the incinerator
    chewing his old vests.

Maternity Ward

Since the new mother, cross and tired,
    has gone to sleep early,
    he leaves the darkened room,
    and takes the long hall to the nursery,
    past tiny bulbs along the wall
    set just at cut-off distance,
    shadows crocheting them together,
    a milky-blue expanse.

The elevator goes up to the top,
    where people die, he knows,
    where men push muffled mops
    not to wake ears from dying,
    where room lights are turned off,
    maybe forever,
    waiting for the bright blank burst of light
    that comes with death.

Here, in a slumber of creation,
    the pulsing whites reflect all pallors.
Glass panels screen from him
    the soft handfuls of bodies,
    so recently part of another body,
    and still half dormant, on their sterile trays,
    diapered amphibians, panting gently,
    globose.
Vapors and shadows flicker: thin,
    terminal grandfathers vaporizing;
    new nebulae gathering, slowly,
    a maze of motes.
A nurse dreams through her graveyard-shift schedule
    in this time-marriage. Our flesh
    delivers ghosts.

Dry Nights

In the dry dusk,
safe, soundless lightning,
their hope of rain,
flashed in the west,
flicked at the August porch,
and then receded
writing silently,
a snaking pencil
on clouds miles away.

Schoolgirls, we
detached us from them, we
charged insistently
from lamps and porch,
charged blackness,
ordered a terra nova
through the unmapped clouds,

while they
sat in the young dark,
one in the swing,
one back to column,
disclosing twosome what they'd thought,
all day, one in the house,
one far afield:
some unearthed atom of their childhoods,
some brooded yield,
some duet silence,
casting, now and then
into the dark:
    Don't go too far.
    Don't stumble on a snake.

Rain never came, as I remember—
never comes,

and we, most lost,
are compassed looking back
at those two sitting there
half darkness and half lightning
in our night.

No

Who will meet her?
    sitting ahead of me,
    her face a crushed girlskin,
    her head rotating
    almost acceptably, as if she were
    just looking out west windows on the bus,
    then out east ones and back,
    a run of negatives—?
Has her world changed out-and-out?
Or has she lived bound to some weird set-up—
    the mule that's dragged the wheel
    till it can only circumscribe,
    and at a straight path must be led?

What doctor sanctioned this furlough?
Can she be circling alone?

Her hair, an edgeless haze.
Under the cotton shell, a stance
    wandlike, almost airborne.
She rises now and then compelled
    to seem to look out windows,
    her face unseeing; frets with
    her large dark purse and, at her feet,
    black plastic trash bag with twist tie.

Within her trance she's spotted
    free seats across from me;
    deserts a sleeping Mexican,
    taking her plastic bag,
    to sit alone.

Her garment's flowered; her soles
    inside flat sandals, old rubber
    weathered to chapped rose.

She takes off twist-it, rapt;
 opens the bag, peers in,
 cautiously shifting things, removing nothing,
 arm elbow deep, like one engaged in calving;
 takes out—can it be, more folded plastic bags
 blistered with use? . . . *Not those.*
And something coarse and white—dish towels?
Change of underwear? *Not that.*
She is alone, absorbed
 she's in some way-off house,
 a mansion long devoid of lords;
 or a big empty room
 with towering windows—
 even a small empty room—
 alone, so alone one wonders
 where she is going TO, who
 has room enough for that loneliness, that quiet.
Yet—not where is she going,
but where she came from—

Now she slides out a worn,
 staghandled paring knife.
The thin blade's longish.
She drifts it out and puts it by,
 restores the bags and piece of cloth,
 fastens the twist-it patiently,
 then moves back to the Mexican.
By now he's taken over her seat, too.
She almost sits on him.
He jumps awake, his look a reprimand.

Remotely. . . . *'cuse.* . . . Then
 her being seems to vanish.
Her head repeats its back-and-forth.
The knife rides in the seat across from me
 in independent menace.

I check the other passengers,
    the ones who turn and eye her anxiously,
    for one in charge of her.
Perhaps the Mexican's her keeper.
He seems to feel no threat.
Abruptly she investigates her skirt,
    looks quickly backward to the seat she left,
    not rising, reaches back,
    arm stretching crazily
    till like a magnet it's pulled in the knife.
She draws it to her lap, sits straight (*that's done*)
    becomes again the metronome
    that drums no tune—
    no
    no
    no

Hatchways

Sleeping rapidly
    I climb desperately
    a hatchway mercilessly
    narrow-channeled. . . .
    or else a slimy chimneypot
    my toehold crumbling
    as I twist up

    that offers,
    (if I get through)
           a fatal ledge
    hung over deluged plains,
    no roads there, sea snapping—

Where did this terror come from?
this twitching like despair?
I whose birth was
"the easiest one"
who came fast and simply—I
have no need for such nightmares.

Did some drowned sailor
drifting in race memory, on
some not-as-yet-known electrothought,
chance up in me,
rebuking his hard fate?

Or some wretch in my family past,
too far back for my tale-tellers
to reach back to, come navigate
my sleep,
and wring his trauma out?
rise jinni in my blood?
say that he's me?

Or is that
soon-to-be-born
blood of my blood,
two hundred miles away,
gathering his-or-her strength
(mixed with mine)
on the private, drowsy
sea of amnion,
something like thought
disturbing its red cobweb:
    No choice now.
    Only the job that all flesh must—
he-or-she summoning
our strength for being hurled
through the dread channel to
the raw bite of the world?

Or a black foreshadow
of my shade,
me waking blind
inside strange blood
next century,
mute,
laboring to get the ear
of some deaf, stubborn,
all-enclosing metamorph:
I'm here, here   *?*

Pain in the House

Feeling her head pick up her body,
    question mark,
    blurred misstamped question mark
    snakes out of bed,
    trying to jiggle unhappiness
    as little as possible,
    not to wake pain,
    not to raise a shade,
    if raising a shade in the dark wakes pain.
Under the shade the stars are awake, smiling—
    ready to frown on unhappiness.
And the happiness of the unconscious
    is scurrying already
    from the knife-edge of light,
    pain's night-light,
    waiting under the door across the hall.
Dread's square hair stiffens,
    her feet have corners,
    trying to trick the stairs out of their creaking,
    and the house out of groaning before coffee,
    before resurrection.
Death before resurrection is hard ;
    breakfast and the stars belong first ;
    plenty of time to die all day
    when everything does groan, and unhappiness
    shakes itself out like a musty old mare
    all over the house.
Dread says to herself : Serves me right
    for leaving home, for learning to read ;
    serves me right for children and menopause
    and cosmetic surgery, and elation in gin.
              I must travel back
    through the shade and the black holes and the frowns,

through drink and tampon and alphabet
to the kitchen and mother and dad and
the morning of the resurrection was the first day.

Next Year

everything will be bigger :
six-inch growth on rhododendrons,
        green leather,   hide of embryo;
every pine a foot further up the sky;
sweet woodruff,   sidling among bulbs
        as if unthoughtup

there will be more money :
no need to check the tag
        on nursery potlings;
I'll have the 10 ft. thorn
to bloom the first year,
        a tree before I'm old

I will know more :
the disillusion of camellia
        the afterthought of invasives
the reserved judgment of bone meal;
I'll be a black forest of folk wisdom
        floored with green cones

there will be more time :
my engagement book blank
        but for numerals,   sixteen, seventeen, eighteen;
no unscheduled absences,   the names of the months
in unhurried sequence :
        January is waiting,
the others are busy
uncalendrically,
        May for example is raking,
she's collecting brown leaves like moisture,
preparing a wayside
        where schemes may fall

the weather will be better :   drought ending;
rain,   rain flying up from the SW
    will dangle blowing
against my loved porch
blowing in on the porch
    spattering the empty rocking chairs
swelling their dead wood
like embalming fluid

I won't miss the ducks' migration :
stepping into the night by my gate I'll hear
    the appointed skytramping,
the comradely call; who knows?
it may be my year to share
    the vacant eye full of destination

Late Leisure

(1999)

Long-Dreaded Event Takes Place

it blurs
        happening as on canvas
distanced
        almost out of earshot
                moving unwillingly
in galactic impulse
        not touching me
                crawling   as I
remote, half turned away,
        my eyes half-closed
                half watch,

a painter   at my easel
        distancing my sketch
                pretending I recede

not present
        hoping   hoping
                I'm not present
glazed eyes catching
        small smithereens:
                the nurse's ring
bone pink smooth though modified
        the brief convulsive reflex
                and the driver's shoes well tied

everything establishes
        my absence in this scene
                later somewhere
I'll paint-in gaps, fill in
        the larger picture,
                withholdings spilled
out of my pockets of resistance—
        the brushes
                the paints
the skill

Diary Entry, March 24

Today
walked home tho cold
No coffee no Crackerjack no
books $200 cash 3.50 taxi
saved 5.69 coffee not spent
           Wind blowing
hard Scarf tossing in my face
breathing fast the cold
A young man boy walking
like that boy in Ellerbe hands deep
in pockets shoulders twisting
          mouth bitter
glittering eyes black-fringed into looking
Kiss-me-quick-I'm-off-goodbye tied
my scarf under my chin
         Hurry
Just past the bridge wind threw
a foam hot dog carton onto
the walk ahead of me It landed
flat waddled along open a little casket
determined to get home first But
the wind lifted it again took it off I,
determined to get there before it
         Waddle
as the wind blows, casket
       A fling
of maple keys to street
That's the way the money goes
Keys eyes bluegray Black-fringed

Don't shiver little star
It's not as cold as all that

Overgrown Path

Having rebought a fragment of the past
   I tear my way back through
the path I gardened years ago.
   Are these the things I planted?
Laurel head-high, snarled with kudzu.
   You've got it back.
Daffs, in runs, not blooming
   under ten years' leaves.
Re-do the works.
   The single multiflora I "might allow"
is the upper hand, lassos the foot.
   Trim canopy for light. No bulbs. Fill in.

   A dirging crash.
   Somewhere in umbrage,
   a dead branch, letting go:

      In here
      is
      1989.
      Somewhere,
      the day
      I scuttled Benedict.
      The afternoon I missed my train
      and went back to their icy eyes.
      The night—

No bulbs. Fill in. Plant-over
all this noxious mess of bramble roots.

Completing the Pilgrimage

A stubborn foxgray shack.
One bending oak too claybound to fall down.
    Here the schoolbus turned
    and went back to the world.

We watched nine children exit headlong,
    tear off three ways . . .
                    their dens.

All, my mother said, in this backwoods
    some kin to me.
    The idiot brother. The crazy uncle, too.
The white-browed figure
    in a black plush
    hat off some Colonial shelf,
there sometimes, stockstill
    as his stick . . .
                    some kin.

Two miles back
    we'd left the road,
    gone through a trestle, down
a tunnel fringe-trees and wild bloom,
    huffing at the wheels.
    Bumps and splashes. Birds
unaccustomed scudding off the lane.
    Hounds sleeping around washpots
    black-nosed, sleep-deprived.
The house in which our Civil War
    deserted kin made good his hide.

Sometimes the student driver
    intoned archly: "All out for
    Kimmerville!" for the benefit of Kimreys
who never took a book home,
    walked off with every prize.

I liked going through the tunnel twice.
When we re-did the trestle, climbed
   back up to home road, day joined us
   where we'd left it. Rote fences
and home houses flicked by
   like TV frames, not yet invented.

In my Platonic heaven I too get off the bus.
   It rounds the longing tree,
   no danger to the foxgray steps,
then snails back toward warm
   quilts and milk, is gone

I break and run for Kimmerville.

Te Deum

Lord
    sho been good to me

      My loved hoe handle, and my sweat,
heart pounding and the towhee singing.

    Jill, jerking the hospital sheets,
      "Damn careless nurses . . .
"But golly . . . a good life.
     "That student who kept writing me.
       "That rainy picnic by a road in Burgundy.
"Heart thumping, thumping on . . . more, more. . . ."

     A squirrel on a post.
The nutgrooved skull
    drops; he claws the dirt.
     Next winter!
Frost thrown down,
    a stiffened morning,
      a harsh corrective herb
to gnaw, take in.

    Sho been, Lord, Sho been

     Whether born of kiss sublime,
victim's terror, rapist crime, and
    however ending,
      nut-gnawers nulled
inscrutably, or
    Caesars,
     soldiers, friends
lammed open-eyed—

    Lord, good . . . sho been

The Lighthouse Keeper

The car lights wake me
   in the dark at five,
    the long beams in the next drive
cruising my hinterland,
the safe slip of my single bed.
   It is the lighthouse keeper I half
    dream, bringing the beams
home with her for the day,
into her mama's kitchen
   or garage with her old skis.
                    Some day
snipping at the sink
   she'll hack them short
   and spike them in a vase
for her window. They'll blink.
Beware, missing husband, dropout
   kids, pro tem moonlight job.

Find Me

by my trail of fragments,
                                                      stale crumbs,

        green broken boughs
            of protocol.
                    Footprints
all missteps,

        tatters of sackcloth
            on the undergrowth,

confused backtracks.
            A rough HELP
lipsticked on a map
        tossed out too far
                with backbite cream.
                                        Here

left the highway

        for the woods
pressed jungleward.   Discover

        a trace of desiccated residue
                staining a sheet of paper

struggling to speak.

The Accidental Prisoner

Will anybody find me
under my own back porch?
I cut some sprigs of mint, then
ducked in here to check
the dryer vent. The door swung-to
and clicked. At one slam,
under everything, porch floor
and kitchen, 911, my empty house.
The neighbors in their shrubs
conjectural.
        A Bastille
daylight lattices this cell.

I think I left a burner on.
Could firemen hear me
above the basso
of their radios?
Will I get thirsty? Miss lunch?
One could relieve oneself,
there's privacy.
        A bunch
of stained, chipped flowerpots.
Clay saucers. Some unaccountable
bright straw. A bag of ossified
Sakrete to sit on,
if one could sit.
Trapped possums pace.

Come on. The door's just lattice.
One hinge is even loose.

My banging with a stone
bruises my thumbnail till it bleeds.
It hurts. *Loose* isn't *weak*.

Nobody comes. . . .
Prisoners do tunnel under. . . .

      Last summer we drove by our cemetery,
      admiring its retired antiquity,
      its roses shrouding bony trellises,
      so musical with texts and poetry,
      so in demand, the next
      lot's been annexed—a glaring
      scrub with stubblefield
      and one or two slick slabs. . . .

I could have washed these pots
and filled them with rosemary.

Nota bene, my survivors: I'm to be buried
in the old part of the cemetery.

O Lamp

After tornado wrenched
our cabin out of line
my father rebuilt down the hill
a reeking bungalow, new pine,
three chimneys, and a high front porch.

My mother moved the lamps.
Now, walk behind me, babe.
Both in our coats. Down the dirt road,
glass font well up, firm hands around its waist,
its see-through, brass-clipped chimney tight,
its unlit wick looped dreamily in oil.

Winter sun. No flame. We walk.
She is ahead. I follow. I keep following.

There seems a light there,
seems some glint,
something blazed in print;
some shadow from her hands,
not from the sun.
This has gone on so long
the lamp's grown to her arm,
the arm is a relic,
the light's dropped back, it's
changed its residence.

The Diary

1

Too much like myself,
it listens critically.
Edits, though seldom rereads.
In the margins: *here incoherent.*

Like me, it mumbles.
The more I "Speak up, girl!"
the less it says outright,
wants in fact to not say.

2

Contrary to belief, the word *diary*
means undivulged; clues trail
the pages and the trail breaks off,
scent's lost. Wandering is
the only way out of this place.

Yet the helpless subjugation
to the daily task,
the need for trysting-place,
love for the white-hot page
that drains the wound, seals it.

3

I know the heroines of the craft—
the small-town wife, the *clear some,
cloudy some* fretful refrain
in her doubtful second marriage;
Jane Carlyle's war with crowing cocks.

To whom? To me. They write to me.
From pages hidden in the covered wagon,
"I said nothing, but I thought the more."

(But in a letter home:
"We are at the mercy of a madman.")
Missing, Fanny Kemble's account
of the night she fled upriver.

4

How to confide the footsteps of a shroud
under your window in the night?
The denials, the costumed felons
lurk in your wakings, nervously
pressing mustaches over their teeth.

Why are those scuds of gulls
hanging over the swamp today?

I, splashing, choking, struggling,
sinking in self-sight—

Oh, that little straw!

These Gifts

Fred Ross, 1913–1993

We take nothing out of this world

except yarns you invented at
   the feedsack that fed the planter
   as it worked in the pear-tree field
   minding small sibling in straw hat,
except the willow at the springhead
   you dug out (home for the funeral I saw only
   workers pouring out of Textiles-Cone),
the non-curricular you majored
   in   your rabbit boxes   bantam
   Easter egg that outpipped
   all your cousins',
your silly melon crop that   green-
   streaked hogs   wallowed branchside
   your gun where is it? and the squirrels
   you toppled out of trees and ate fried,
your diary's secrets (rouged schoolgirls
   trailed me down the playground:
   "Tell Fra-yed—I love him!"),
   the banjo that you swapped a jacket
   for then yo-lee-lay-hooed to
   on front steps at dusk,

the empties clinking in your desk
   among the last abandoned novel's
   pages (music that knows that winning loses),
except your grim voice miles away
   after my *You spend your day*—?:
   Waiting for dark!
even last year's tall skeletal
   smile that took me by the hand
   never a *Mayday mayday* from the stark

porch's canes and
                         calendars wherein
our parents called down
to the last one up *Be sure*
to put the fire to bed;

you take your cache that flares and flashes
    out   a recent breath.

Last Ant

They scutter in my dreams, the ants
that left the flower pot,
    that third plant
    I watched die, one of three
basils rescued from the freeze.
A fungus or mildew.
    I had to pull it up
    and leave the soil to dry.

Then ants began to come out,
cross the crater, the dusty
    desert of old potting soil;
    every appendage twitching, they explored
the great clay wall,
the width of plastic saucer,
    white longitude of sill,
mad for a jot to drink.
The natural thing to do was kill them all.

This morning, one more ant
ran wildly—he knew where?—
a straight line toward the sink.

Someone at the University
might take his questions:
    why there's no rainfall
    anymore, what happened to his
habitat, how Edens dry
up suddenly—in short, why
    he's endangered—things
    in his compound eyes not simple.

I gave the coup de grâce,
a little overkill (his bony suit)
    before I took the pot outside,
    and washed my hands.

Always Reclusive,

I'm constructing my own brierpatch. True,
I'm still bleeding from the first canes I dug in;
thorns fight off cultivation, cut both ways;
they like barbwiring things in
as much as battling guests; that's useful;
I won't try getting out too soon, say for a
tipsy fruit, or reckless stroll. What I don't spend
on tickets I'll apply on long long-distance calls.

Hunters will come and shake my fence, dogs panting,
paws pointing. I'll like that. I'll cuddle up
and turn the page.

"The blackberry, permitted its own way,
is an unmanageable plant." Here's a
variety called *Taylor:* "Season late,
bush vigorous, hardy . . . free from rust."
That's it. Don't let my brierpatch rust.

Converse

I'm a woman at a window
talking to a man outside.
                    My elbow's
on the sill. The carved
        acanthus leaves
        behind me wheeze
with dust.
        Some other leaves
crush
        underneath his shoes
        flat on the canvas
(you can't hear this of course).

The artist has two guises
in one time
and so must I.

Pretend a 16-wheeler
                    booms
past just out of frame,
rattling long emptiness
on our moot commune.
Then say I know this man:
(I, she) Where the dust of the day
        meets the dust of the night.
(He) Don't be decadent.
(I, she) Right.

In the room behind me, in
the real house I stand in,
a voice rises and falls
                    in paints,
separates in parts:
                    somebody—
it's that man

pitched back to life,
                    I can
tell by his eyes
(which you'll never see—
                    they're shaded
in, averted, as if autistic,
                    and they're dead).
But he's still playing
rending variations on a tune
after cicadas,
a summer's ending,
                    the summer's ending,
that summer's ending.

I take it up, humming,
or have taken it up.

He stands before me. But I
don't listen. Why
am I humming?
                    I'm humming.

And
never having heard
my voice from a distance
I turn my ear
                    softly
back into the picture

acritically. Do I like
      what I hear?
Shall I hum? Or sing
      out clear?

Cocoon

He's in intensive care, a coma,
the neighbor I lunched with last month,
astonished, still, his house
so nondescript outside
was lined with years of
vintage craved by Christie's:
with prints and serried maps
in frames he made himself
(hours of mitered molding
and distressed hand-rubbing);

woodwork he made himself,
his delicate long hands
guiding the saw, tacking
the molding into panels
to dress up doors, making old
mantels to match one really old;
folding, above the salvaged lead-glass
window lugged from England,
a red silk valance shot and
fringed with gold, flickering
out tarnished earls and witches;

painted kings and Buddhas
staring from four walls,
pop-eyed stitches in past time
weirdly transported, transmitted,
transmogrified, implanted in his house,
his nest, his chrysalis, his semidormant,
nightclothes, saw-toothed dream.

Yes, I expect any hour now.

Kitchen Fable

The fork lived with the knife
    and found it hard—for years
took nicks and scratches,
    not to mention cuts.

She who took tedium by the ears:
    nonforthcoming pickles,
defiant stretched-out lettuce,
    sauce-gooed particles.

He who came down whack.
His conversation, even, edged.

Lying beside him in the drawer
    she formed a crazed patina.
The seasons stacked—
    melons, succeeded by cured pork.

He dulled; he was a dull knife,
while she was, after all, a fork.

Late Leisure

Some things achieve finale;
vivace to larghetto;
three hundred pages, *End;*
threescore and ten, of course,
    that's it.

But this embroidery that I
inch aimlessly along
could be found years from now
wadded unfinished
    in a basket.

I, past my expiration date,
fold the cloth twice for center,
my needle threaded for the first
small stitch, myself
    capriciously ongoing.

I see it, as a sampler, challenging.
It has a long, protracted feel—
the dog each morning barking at the gate,
just where I left him
    yesterday.

I'll flesh out by the millimeter
a gawky shepherdess,
a time-lapse Federal house beyond,
odd birds and fish to signify
    earth floundering on,

the alphabet that's used
for English, French, Italian—
more tongues than I will speak
in this life, but fewer than birdcalls
    I recognize.

I'll work through color changes
almost photosynthetic;
I'll search out chairs by windows
in south-facing rooms;
    I'll never work by artificial light.

The sun won't cast a shadow of these men.
The curly beasts submit to cubist life
as in some static dream
the dead dream in their sleep,
    some plastic intervention.

If I get to the last rows
of this kit, I'll have to find
another one as slow and interim;
    but no need plan that yet.

New Poems

(1999–2008)

When to Stop

Never knew when to stop, my Aunt Estelle.
A girl, called to recite
(a thing she did quite well)
she waxed so eloquent,
went on so long,
her Papa growled, "Oh, let up, Stell!"

Kept up, past forty,
singing lessons with Miss Gottschalk;
at seventy-five still clings
to artless, low-cut blouse,
lipsticks the retrograding mouth.

I've seen her (in-laws
envying her prelude seafood stems,
half-scornful of her postlude fingerbowls)
presiding at her table,
erect and smiling, answering
her husband's snarl
with a quick nimble joke
that gave us all escape.

Now he has nothing more
to say to her, to tired-out us,
or to the world,
when he just leans his forehead
hard upon his hand, and
nully forks and chews.
A living silence, she, erect and smiling,
giving his sleeve a quick caress,
eyes like a cherubim's,
chats on voraciously for two.

Three Days in Flower

Monday he went away.

The moon was in her sign,
the weather smiled,
she cut Jacques Cartiers,
thornless,
pink as in holiday.

From a champagne flute
they waved intimate,
buds opened,
centers fulfilled;
she dreamed in their arms,
cloud and city,
music swelled.

Thursday
one wrinkled, mauved,
one sang alone,
one threatened suicide
on glass-topped table.

He flew home.

Transience

I join in anonymity of robins at sundown,
dark, interchangeable, in perch on bedroom tree.
Six at a time alight, rise, go for a fly,
return, their eggs unknown, their fledglings gone,
eyeing, significantly, at the window, me.

They have no names; only, for the night,
footage where nails can cling
and eyelids close. . . .
They don't count hours.
No recollection
of a sun that rose.
Alarmed, watch sun slink out
under its one black wing.

This day, a drill in the ephemeral,
gives up the ghost.
"We—you—" the robins pantomime:
"expect the same."
Through falling dark, while I still can,
I call out to
my own old tucked-in emigrants by name.

Lawrence at the Etruscan Tombs

He swaggers with feverish grin,
    frail tyrant rasping at the guides:
To the tombs! Now!
    (Rude opener of cans of worms,
young addict of the female clasp.)

    A stiff dog, sunning, shakes himself *No,*
sighs; men descend
    into a night, a cold.
Down, down dirt steps the lanterns gutter;
    flame unsheaths tufa beams,
furls out redbody and blacklock—
    Rise! laced foot on a wakened road!
A syrinx cry of *Battle.* . . .

Tuberculoidal fervor rakes dead walls
    room after room: Freedom's big-eyed stare?
blind servitude? majestically
    the painted shades unfurl,
struck by his brandished light:
    goddesses horseback, bright caustic worlds—
tombed collieries?

Old heroes bat their eyes,
    wrench hands loose from the paint
to shade their sight—
    waked in this shafted night
disturbed, transfused,
    with David's short long glory.

The Dead

Like germs
they grow more virulent
in slumber,
commanding the pillow
to remember the dream.

Aroused, they set their teeth
and pound the stairs,
writs of the past on feverish tongues.

The night ogres hum
Let me call you sweetheart.
The letter boxes—dusty,
envelopes—corrupt.

Wind blowing all afternoon,
a soft roar that might be
water at great distance falling
into river rapids.

A self-occupied voice—
Going there, going there, going there—
Icy breath from something without lungs.
A soldier carrying the lost loved face.

Gift

Gift snubs artist,
lives its own life,
sometimes in the same room with
its human habitation,
sometimes wandering alone
on empty streets,

or searching its host's fridge,
opening the door that lights up
what lives in darkness,
on hold in case of hunger:

its writ to gnaw, to grow,
eat artist out of house and home.

Two Poems for Randall Jarrell

R.J.

The meteor loosed
from the council of worlds
flashes and cartwheels through
pure emptiness,
burns itself out
in earth's atmosphere,
too dingy, cacophonous
for its ear's anapest.

THE LOST BOY

He was an old-fashioned bear.
Was he a bear?
He was just a boy, really—
Peter Pan—and one day
when the mirror gave him
the gray in his beard
and cheeks, too, he said
I'll none of that.

O lost world and lost boy
(you only bear reading)

October

All summer, longing for his winter sleep,
stretching and upright, chewing berries,
thinks of
      no chewing, no lookout
for trouble, any species.
Sun's—hot. Breeze—dries the eyes.
The stream fibs, telling rainbows.
Fur and claws groomed daily seem
curling and softening into quilt and pillow.
  Wade stream. Climb stairs.
  Balance checkbook.
  Berries fall. Leaves blanket lawn.
  In front of me's
  the underworld's dark maw.
  I greet it with a predatory yawn.

How to Live in a Trap

First, drag yourself and
   that whole thing
     down to a waterhole,
under some hastate leaves, if possible.
   They'll also serve
     as ambush for food-gathering
if you use skill,
   keep your pain quiet,
     and don't reek of blood.
A little dew could help.
   Stars, too.
     Refrain from gnawing.
At the right stage of corruption
   wrest the steel teeth
     from the softer flesh.
You'll hear the wren sing
   procedure, procedure, proceed.
     If you pass out, dream a few days.
Lick wounds regularly.
   Practice deep breathing at scheduled
   intervals.
Tell yourself there's a painting
   in this somewhere:
     Interior, Woman Singing.

Our Lives Are Rounded with a Sleep

Katherine Taylor, 1948–2001

Where are they sleeping,
the babies to be born
a hundred years from now?

Where did she sleep, my daughter,
when I was a child?

Has she gone back?
    And will she know the place?
      Who's there?
Or does it matter who is there,
in that blank space?

In fluid form?
Force without form?
    Her tiny nails, her lustrous hair,
    her laughing face.

Survivor on a sofa, I
re-voyage to window's trees,
likes ones where I was new—
    their swing, their girls, their words—
    and watch night fall.

Return from there—
    A There that was a place?
    Where is it now?

Her nails, her heavy hair,
(her pillowed face)

Disappearing Act

No, soul doesn't leave the body.

My body is leaving my soul.
Tired of turning fried chicken and
coffee to muscle and excrement,
tried of secreting tears, wiping them,
tired of opening eyes on another day,
tired especially of that fleshy heart,
pumping, pumping. More,
that brain spinning nightmares.
Body prepares:
disconnect, unplug, erase.

But here, I think, a smallish altercation
arises.
Soul seems to shake its fist.
Wants brain? Claims dreams and nightmares?
Maintains a codicil bequeathes it shares?

There'll be a fight. A deadly struggle.
We know, of course, who'll win. . . .

But who's this, watching?

I See Nobody

A knock. The I I live with disappears.
   Unlike Narcissus, I reject the wrinkled hand
     of that dull looking-glass: we two,
  I and the one I cook for.
    But readily concede
  Half could turn to
    a dog, or paid companion, new two.

A knock.
  We, solitaire, erratic, given to long
    living in and looking out,
  draped in lank ells of unused time,
    blind hours and dates,
  silences, short whistles—

a knock, my odd charge disappears;
  ells turn to clothes,
    my silence comes to life,
  pupil absents herself, and
    teacher quickly leafs to
  hollow, stagnant, faceless speech.

Laughter

Your wadded pillow.
     Baleful, lighted dial.
Your only stars:
     a leaky roof, a traffic fine, those files.

Across the hall:
     youth bed, bars down,
          night light.
Suddenly your child laughs in her sleep.
     An outburst wholly belly:
hilarity spontaneous whirlwinds
     down the hall into your door
hits you head-on non sequitur, carefree,

She's playing Follow Wallaby—
     Here comes Dad sabertooth
on hands and knees. . . .

Silence sags back.

Laugh? You laugh?
     That wallaby has fists.
You'll pay that fine. Roof leaks.
     Daylight's no joke.

Eve

The serpent in my Eden
swallowed Adam.
He slithered into meals;
of course, my bed.
Wrapped himself tighter, tighter,
all around me,
ejecting sweetish venom
in my head,
no simple adder.
That stupe's gone, he said,
strangling,
love me instead.

Born Alpha

Zora Neale Hurston, Greensboro, N.C., 1939

Using only the letter Alpha,
convert a shack into a belvedere.
Half pine, half palm.
Half gift, half waste.

Using only the letter Alpha
raise a goddess in a desert.
Sands blow and storms half bury.

    You rise laughing. Stand

        flat against our parlor wall,
        all Alpha.
        Decline our tea, smiling a bit
        beneath your pillbox veil,
        smoothing gloved hands.

        Your fierce transcendence
        made ashes of
        our girls' Quill Club.
        Bearing our brand ruefully
        we still petition Time,
        thirsting for tea with Alpha.

Imago Mundi

David Wilkie's *Christopher Columbus in the Convent of La Rábida Explaining His Intended Voyage* (1834)

The prophecy in their faces and
that present they are grouped in,
both history now as much
as Spain's world power,
the lure of ocean sails,
dreams of Cathay.

The Discoverer's stance
and gaze not unlike one
writing the first sentence
of an inspired text
or setting down
the first line of a poem,
but not with pen, with compass
lantern-light picks up
and seems to move,
an automatic writing,
fate drafting history.

He halted in despair,
becalmed in his firm course,
this man of destiny,
"in person tall and shapely,"
at anchor with the monks;
wrote his own prayer
to "Him who created
heaven, earth, and sea."

Confessor to the Queen,
in shadow, plots
the decked ship and two caravels,
the royal letter to the Great Khan
of Cathay. Does he foreknow

the meteor that will fall into the sea
the eighth day into voyage? A sign
from God? Approving? Or indifferent?
Does he already wonder if it means
a second voyage with missionaries
and more boats (that carried back
five shiploads of bound Indians,
sold in Seville as slaves)?

Young Ferdinand stares, lost:
his hands, forgetful of
what he is holding—his bread?
his top?—already

relics of young appetite,
his child's eyes feverish
with old seamen's tales. . . .
"Men fancied that there hove in sight . . ."
the secret of the Western seas,
the mystery of Aztec sacrifice.
The rough pirogues that Lewis took,
with whiskey, no missionaries, no
fur-trimmed robes for greeting a Great Khan.

They are conjecturing
figures we've seen transmute
and disappear, they dream
of distances that exhaust
explorers, exhaust geographers.

They dream of us.
One frightened face, half
darkness, sees all to be
given up along the way:
the ships storm-crippled;
the wives in wagon trains,
racing winter: "Today threw out
the old clothes press";

the Trail of Tears, moving slowly,
all things moving Westward.
They're listening to the vast largo
of sea and space; see,
not this world, one new.

Written on their faces,
all theirs not to know:
De Soto's trek through the Rockies;
the landing on the moon;
mechanical Explorers
charting space.

All we are dreaming still,
all still to come of it
gathers in this monastery light
of 1492.

Meanwhile, the 1490s Spanish hound,
head hanging, slinks off
nearer the fire. He knows no
ideal world; he sees Italians,
Spaniards, Indians, and Chinese
a single puzzling species, Man.

Against the Kitchen Wall

A mothball May.
 I lean against the kitchen wall.
 The sacred pear tree on the hill.
 The skyline, small green wheat
 waverunning with the wind.

From west to east the green's
 spanned out by men
 on horseback and on foot,
 men with long staffs
 slow-motion, searching.

The saddles glint.
 What are they sweeping for?
 Why coming this direction?
 Are those staffs guns?

If they are after quail, or hares,
 why is their fanning law-enforcement grim,
 as for a felon, a missing person, or
 one too imbecile to find her way?

One who laid waste
 the safe place by the kitchen wall,
 bankrupted her May day,
 malpracticed pear and gifted wheat?

I'm waiting, men.

Homesick in Paradise

You, light of sunset firing my back fence;
you, wren advising wrens where to bed down,
bypassing, as they close, baled lilies,
stars, inching in;

you, scalloped pillowcases;
you, pale lamp and fat paperback:
no otherworldly life
replaces you, my dreams
of flesh and bivouac.

Eternal peace won't stop
my looking back
to battlefields'
wild bouts of bliss.
No purity makes up for mongrel wags.
How's cloudless sky to thrill
one hooked on storm of human kiss?

I must?
On up this stairway in the flickering light?
    A handrail? . . .
        Squeaky hinge? . . . Up, up. . . . ?
            Goodbye! My ticket's stamped: tonight.

De Facto

The bed says, Come.
We keep on watching Nightline.
My sleep is like a music.
I hear it far away,
as I, Atlantis, sink

dreaming of her past,
dripping her pen in ink.

A road, a house—roads, houses,
dealt by a dream,
shuffled, redealt.
Where're brain's big flimsy boxes?
They hold our houses razed?
years leveled?
unraveled consciousness?
How's big sleep's hollow log?

Who's that joker
shambling behind the liveoak?
My lit professor, fat, his
round gold glasses gleaming? Passing out exams?
Fill in the blanks. Mark true or false, then
date the following.

From a ghost so real
I come back running hard
to the flesh hand beside me,
to household voice
come running,
hear
above ocean's dream:

Your phone's been ringing,
your dog barking,
UPS dropped package.

Wrapping Things Up

Bored with time,
I throw out calendars.
My clocks are dead for sleep.
They're striking—smack sullenly
and growl before each strike.
Their chimes rust in their bowels.

Their timelessness runs down.
Was that a silence I heard strike?
I stagger up, as if of numbers
I had drunk.

Now I'll set out—the night
is lightly starred, sparks
moving micewise without sound.

I am Indians traveling
to new campgrounds.

Star

Mid-night
I was summoned.

Stumbling
in the dark,
raised one shade,
fell on one knee
before star
scrutinizing me
with its one eyepiece.

> Glittering star,
> was it worth it
> from so far
> to find just me?
> You ask for?
> I can bring you?
> Will you come in?

Peering through my window,
from dream risen,
                 recalled
to my page-layered history—
why do I, distraught,
still seek for her
of cradle and sickbed,
among stars, watching?

Payment Past Due

Time has loved me.

How to return time's love?—
love casual and self-interested,
vain of largesse,
all masculine.

Must hatch some souvenir,
though now last-minute . . .
household allowance fund . . .
dress it as can afford,
then wrap up warmly . . .
a basket, too?

leave it, still dreaming,
kicking iambic feet,
always newborn,
at his old, opening door.

Yes?

The dollar mark said
my shoe was long enough
and wide enough and happy
enough which was enough for
me. But it was not enough
for my foot. What did he care
for a happy shoe?
I gave him my left ear.
The right one I kept for
myself and in it I heard

right, right

One Day

One day I'll cry all day,
    the end of it:
Band-Aids, cuts, bruises,
    fingers kissed,
games lost
    on checkered boards
in overtakes,
    queens captured,
kings preoccupied,
    ace hoped for,
but just draw the trey,
    and "Fa' down!" cuts
the Card of Death.
    One day.

Ancestral

Of course, we'll follow.
Did you say horse? or hearse? No matter.
    They're far ahead. They started early,
    shoe buckles, stovepipe hats.

What's triter than hooves' clatter?
Is dead silence worse?
Can't time think anything but _fly_?
(And still won't give us fair goodbye.)

Did you say horse, or hearse?
We listen. No, no calling back.
    We'll follow, yes,
      see petals shatter
and wheels roll over them. No matter.
Bone of our bone,
those old unknowns
who went ahead,
tracked previous blood
and can't turn back
(as if they would).

We can't catch up, to say a word
(far down the line, and traffic's slow).
But, yes, we'll follow, can't say no.